BEST-LOVED BAKING COLLECTION™

Best-Ever COOKIES

America's ★ Best
BRAND-NAME RECIPES®

Pictured on the front cover: Chunky Chocolate Chip Peanut Butter Cookies *(page 22)*.
Pictured on the back cover *(left to right):* Bittersweet Pecan Brownies with Caramel Sauce *(page 74)* and Milk Chocolate Florentine Cookies *(page 26).*

ISBN: 0-8487-2876-9

Library of Congress Control Number: 2004100673

Manufactured in China.

8 7 6 5 4 3 2 1

Microwave Cooking: Microwave ovens vary in wattage. Use the cooking times as guidelines and check for doneness before adding more time.

Preparation/Cooking Times: Preparation times are based on the approximate amount of time required to assemble the recipe before cooking, baking, chilling or serving. These times include preparation steps such as measuring, chopping and mixing. The fact that some preparations and cooking can be done simultaneously is taken into account. Preparation of optional ingredients and serving suggestions is not included.

Contents

chip-chip
hooray

fudgy oatmeal butterscotch cookies

1 package (18.25 ounces) devil's food cake mix
1½ cups quick-cooking or old-fashioned oats, uncooked
¾ cup (1½ sticks) butter, melted
2 large eggs
1 tablespoon vegetable oil
1 teaspoon vanilla extract
1¼ cups "M&M's"® Chocolate Mini Baking Bits
1 cup butterscotch chips

Preheat oven to 350°F. In large bowl combine cake mix, oats, butter, eggs, oil and vanilla until well blended. Stir in "M&M's"® Chocolate Mini Baking Bits and butterscotch chips. Drop by heaping tablespoonfuls about 2 inches apart onto ungreased cookie sheets. Bake 10 to 12 minutes. Cool 1 minute on cookie sheets; cool completely on wire racks. Store in tightly covered container.

Makes about 3 dozen cookies

To avoid overbaking cookies, check them at the minimum baking time. If more time is needed, watch them carefully to make sure they do not overbake. It is better to slightly underbake than overbake cookies.

Top to bottom: *Crispy's Irresistible Peanut Butter Marbles, (page 149), Red's Ultimate "M&M's"® Cookies (page 148), and Fudgy Oatmeal Butterscotch Cookies*

jumbo 3-chip cookies

4 cups all-purpose flour
1 teaspoon baking powder
1 teaspoon baking soda
1½ cups (3 sticks) butter, softened
1¼ cups granulated sugar
1¼ cups packed brown sugar
2 large eggs
1 tablespoon vanilla extract
1 cup (6 ounces) NESTLÉ® TOLL HOUSE® Milk Chocolate
   Morsels
1 cup (6 ounces) NESTLÉ® TOLL HOUSE® Semi-Sweet Chocolate
   Morsels
½ cup NESTLÉ® TOLL HOUSE® Premier White Morsels
1 cup chopped nuts

PREHEAT oven to 375°F.

COMBINE flour, baking powder and baking soda in medium bowl.
Beat butter, granulated sugar and brown sugar in large mixer bowl
until creamy. Beat in eggs and vanilla extract. Gradually beat in flour
mixture. Stir in morsels and nuts. Drop dough by level ¼-cup measure
2 inches apart onto ungreased baking sheets.

BAKE for 12 to 14 minutes or until light golden brown. Cool on
baking sheets for 2 minutes; remove to wire racks to cool completely.

Makes about 2 dozen cookies

hershey®'s "perfectly chocolate" chocolate chip cookies

2¼ cups all-purpose flour
⅓ cup HERSHEY®'S Cocoa
1 teaspoon baking soda
½ teaspoon salt
1 cup (2 sticks) butter or margarine, softened
¾ cup granulated sugar
¾ cup packed light brown sugar
1 teaspoon vanilla extract
2 eggs
2 cups (12-ounce package) HERSHEY®'S Semi-Sweet Chocolate Chips
1 cup chopped nuts (optional)

1. Heat oven to 375°F.

2. Stir together flour, cocoa, baking soda and salt. Beat butter, granulated sugar, brown sugar and vanilla in large bowl on medium speed of mixer until creamy. Add eggs; beat well. Gradually add flour mixture, beating until well blended. Stir in chocolate chips and nuts, if desired. Drop by rounded teaspoons onto ungreased cookie sheet.

3. Bake 8 to 10 minutes or until set. Cool slightly; remove from cookie sheet to wire rack. *Makes about 5 dozen cookies*

peanut butter chip tassies

　　1 package (3 ounces) cream cheese, softened
　　$\frac{1}{2}$ cup (1 stick) butter, softened
　　1 cup all-purpose flour
　　1 egg, slightly beaten
　　$\frac{1}{2}$ cup sugar
　　2 tablespoons butter, melted
　　$\frac{1}{4}$ teaspoon lemon juice
　　$\frac{1}{4}$ teaspoon vanilla extract
　　1 cup REESE'S® Peanut Butter Chips, chopped*
　　6 red candied cherries, quartered (optional)

Do not chop peanut butter chips in food processor or blender.

1. Beat cream cheese and $\frac{1}{2}$ cup butter in medium bowl; stir in flour. Cover; refrigerate about one hour or until dough is firm. Shape into 24 one-inch balls; place each ball into ungreased, small muffin cups ($1\frac{3}{4}$ inches in diameter). Press dough evenly against bottom and sides of each cup.

2. Heat oven to 350°F.

3. Combine egg, sugar, melted butter, lemon juice and vanilla in medium bowl; stir until smooth. Add chopped peanut butter chips. Fill muffin cups $\frac{3}{4}$ full with mixture.

4. Bake 20 to 25 minutes or until filling is set and lightly browned. Cool completely; remove from pan to wire rack. Garnish with candied cherries, if desired.　　　　　　　　　　　　　　*Makes about 2 dozen*

cappuccino spice cookies

2½ teaspoons instant coffee
1 tablespoon boiling water
1 cup butter, softened
1 cup firmly packed light brown sugar
½ cup granulated sugar
2 eggs
1 teaspoon vanilla
2½ cups all-purpose flour
1 teaspoon baking soda
¾ teaspoon cinnamon
¼ teaspoon salt
¼ teaspoon ground cloves
¼ teaspoon ground nutmeg
1½ cups double chocolate chips or semi-sweet chocolate chips
1½ cups cappuccino chips or white chocolate chips

1. Preheat oven to 375°F. Dissolve coffee in water; set aside.

2. Beat butter and sugars in large bowl with electric mixer on medium speed until fluffy. Add eggs, coffee mixture and vanilla; beat until well blended.

3. Combine flour, baking soda, cinnamon, salt, cloves and nutmeg. Gradually add to butter mixture beating at low speed until well combined. Stir in chocolate and cappuccino chips.

4. Drop dough by heaping tablespoonfuls 2 inches apart onto ungreased cookie sheets. Bake 8 to 10 minutes or until set. Let stand on cookie sheets 1 minute; transfer to wire rack; cool completely.

Makes about 3½ dozen cookies

pumpkin spiced and iced cookies

2¼ cups all-purpose flour
1½ teaspoons pumpkin pie spice
1 teaspoon baking powder
½ teaspoon baking soda
½ teaspoon salt
1 cup (2 sticks) butter or margarine, softened
1 cup granulated sugar
1 can (15 ounces) LIBBY'S® 100% Pure Pumpkin
2 large eggs
1 teaspoon vanilla extract
2 cups (12-ounce package) NESTLÉ® TOLL HOUSE® Semi-Sweet
    Chocolate Morsels
1 cup chopped walnuts (optional)
Vanilla Glaze (recipe follows)

PREHEAT oven to 375°F. Grease baking sheets.

COMBINE flour, pumpkin pie spice, baking powder, baking soda and salt in medium bowl. Beat butter and granulated sugar in large mixer bowl until creamy. Beat in pumpkin, eggs and vanilla extract. Gradually beat in flour mixture. Stir in morsels and nuts. Drop by rounded tablespoon onto prepared baking sheets.

BAKE for 15 to 20 minutes or until edges are lightly browned. Cool on baking sheets for 2 minutes; remove to wire rack to cool completely. Spread or drizzle with Vanilla Glaze.   *Makes about 5½ dozen cookies*

vanilla glaze: COMBINE 1 cup powdered sugar, 1 to 1½ tablespoons milk and ½ teaspoon vanilla extract in small bowl; mix well.

chocolate peanut butter chip cookies →

8 (1-ounce) squares semi-sweet chocolate
3 tablespoons butter or margarine
1 (14-ounce) can EAGLE BRAND® Sweetened Condensed Milk
    (NOT evaporated milk)
2 cups biscuit baking mix
1 egg
1 teaspoon vanilla extract
1 cup (6 ounces) peanut butter-flavored chips

1. Preheat oven to 350°F. In large saucepan over low heat, melt chocolate and butter with Eagle Brand; remove from heat. Add biscuit mix, egg and vanilla; with mixer, beat until smooth and well blended.

2. Let mixture cool to room temperature. Stir in peanut butter chips. Shape into 1¼-inch balls. Place 2 inches apart on ungreased baking sheets. Bake 6 to 8 minutes or until tops are lightly crusty. Cool. Store tightly covered at room temperature.   *Makes about 4 dozen cookies*

Prep Time: 15 minutes
Bake Time: 6 to 8 minutes

chocolate chip wafer cookies

½ cup butter, softened
½ cup sugar
1 egg
1 teaspoon vanilla
½ cup all-purpose flour
    Dash salt
1 cup (6 ounces) semisweet chocolate chips
⅓ cup chopped pecans or walnuts

Preheat oven to 350°F. Line cookie sheets with foil; lightly grease foil.

Beat butter and sugar in large bowl until light and fluffy. Add egg; beat until creamy. Stir in vanilla, flour and salt. Add chocolate chips and nuts; mix until well blended. Drop dough by teaspoonfuls 3 inches apart onto prepared cookie sheets.

Bake 7 to 10 minutes or until edges are golden and centers are set. (Cookies are soft when hot, but become crispy as they cool.) Cool completely on foil, then peel foil from cookies.

Makes about 2 dozen cookies

marbled biscotti

$^1/_2$ cup (1 stick) butter or margarine, softened
1 cup granulated sugar
2 large eggs
1 teaspoon vanilla extract
2$^1/_2$ cups all-purpose flour
1 teaspoon baking powder
1 teaspoon baking soda
1$^3/_4$ cups "M&M's"® Chocolate Mini Baking Bits, divided
1 cup slivered almonds, toasted*
$^1/_4$ cup unsweetened cocoa powder
2 tablespoons instant coffee granules

To toast almonds, spread in single layer on baking sheet. Bake at 350°F for 7 to 10 minutes until light golden, stirring occasionally. Remove almonds from pan and cool completely before using.

Preheat oven to 350°F. Lightly grease cookie sheets; set aside. In large bowl cream butter and sugar until light and fluffy; beat in eggs and vanilla. In medium bowl combine flour, baking powder and baking soda; blend into creamed mixture. Dough will be stiff. Stir in 1$^1/_4$ cups "M&M's"® Chocolate Mini Baking Bits and nuts. Divide dough in half. Add cocoa powder and coffee granules to half of the dough, mixing to blend. On well-floured surface, gently knead doughs together just enough to marble. Divide dough in half and gently roll each half into 12×2-inch log; place on prepared cookie sheets at least 4 inches apart. Press remaining $^1/_2$ cup "M&M's"® Chocolate Mini Baking Bits onto outside of both logs. Bake 25 minutes. Dough will spread. Cool logs 15 to 20 minutes. Slice each log into 12 slices; arrange on cookie sheet cut-side down. Bake an additional 10 minutes. (For softer biscotti, omit second baking.) Cool completely. Store in tightly covered container. *Makes 24 pieces*

original nestlé® toll house® chocolate chip cookies

2¼ cups all-purpose flour
1 teaspoon baking soda
1 teaspoon salt
1 cup (2 sticks) butter or margarine, softened
¾ cup granulated sugar
¾ cup packed brown sugar
1 teaspoon vanilla extract
2 large eggs
2 cups (12-ounce package) NESTLÉ® TOLL HOUSE® Semi-Sweet
   Chocolate Morsels
1 cup chopped nuts

PREHEAT oven to 375°F.

COMBINE flour, baking soda and salt in small bowl. Beat butter, granulated sugar, brown sugar and vanilla extract in large mixer bowl until creamy. Add eggs, one at a time, beating well after each addition. Gradually beat in flour mixture. Stir in morsels and nuts. Drop by rounded tablespoon onto ungreased baking sheets.

BAKE for 9 to 11 minutes or until golden brown. Cool on baking sheets for 2 minutes; remove to wire racks to cool completely.

Makes about 5 dozen cookies

pan cookie variation: GREASE 15×10-inch jelly-roll pan. Prepare dough as above. Spread into prepared pan. Bake for 20 to 25 minutes or until golden brown. Cool in pan on wire rack. Makes 4 dozen bars.

slice and bake cookie variation: PREPARE dough as above. Divide in half; wrap in wax paper. Refrigerate for 1 hour or until firm. Shape each half into 15-inch log; wrap in wax paper. Refrigerate for 30 minutes. (Dough may be stored in refrigerator for up to 1 week or in freezer for up to 8 weeks.) Preheat oven to 375°F. Cut into ½-inch-thick slices; place on ungreased baking sheets. Bake for 8 to 10 minutes or until golden brown. Cool on baking sheets for 2 minutes; remove to wire racks to cool completely. Makes about 5 dozen cookies.

chunky chocolate chip peanut butter cookies

1¼ cups all-purpose flour
½ teaspoon baking soda
½ teaspoon ground cinnamon
½ teaspoon salt
¾ cup (1½ sticks) butter or margarine, softened
½ cup packed brown sugar
½ cup granulated sugar
½ cup creamy peanut butter
1 large egg
1 teaspoon vanilla extract
2 cups (12-ounce package) NESTLÉ® TOLL HOUSE® Semi-Sweet
    Chocolate Morsels
½ cup coarsely chopped peanuts

PREHEAT oven to 375°F.

COMBINE flour, baking soda, cinnamon and salt in small bowl. Beat butter, brown sugar, granulated sugar and peanut butter in large mixer bowl until creamy. Beat in egg and vanilla extract. Gradually beat in flour mixture. Stir in morsels and peanuts.

DROP dough by rounded tablespoon onto ungreased baking sheets. Press down slightly to flatten into 2-inch circles.

BAKE for 7 to 10 minutes or until edges are set but centers are still soft. Cool on baking sheets for 4 minutes; remove to wire racks to cool completely.   *Makes about 3 dozen cookies*

nancy's dishpan cookies

2 Butter Flavor CRISCO® Sticks or 2 cups Butter Flavor CRISCO®
    all-vegetable shortening plus additional for greasing
2 cups firmly packed light brown sugar
2 eggs
1 tablespoon vanilla
2 cups all-purpose flour
2 cups oats (quick or old-fashioned, uncooked)
1 teaspoon salt
1 teaspoon baking soda
1 teaspoon ground cinnamon
2 cups semisweet chocolate chips
1²/₃ cups butterscotch chips
2 cups large pecan halves

1. Heat oven to 375°F. Grease baking sheet with shortening. Place sheets of foil on countertop for cooling cookies.

2. Combine shortening and brown sugar in very large bowl. Beat at medium speed of electric mixer until well blended. Beat in eggs and vanilla.

3. Combine flour, oats, salt, baking soda and cinnamon. Add gradually to creamed mixture at low speed. Finish mixing with spoon. Stir in chocolate chips, butterscotch chips and nuts. Fill ice cream scoop that holds ¼ cup with dough, rounding slightly (or use ¼-cup measure). Drop 3 inches apart onto prepared baking sheet.

4. Bake at 375°F for 12 to 15 minutes or until light brown and just set. *Do not overbake.* Cool 2 minutes on baking sheet. Remove cookies to foil to cool completely.   *Makes about 2½ dozen cookies*

milk chocolate florentine cookies

²/₃ cup butter
2 cups quick oats
1 cup granulated sugar
²/₃ cup all-purpose flour
¼ cup light or dark corn syrup
¼ cup milk
1 teaspoon vanilla extract
¼ teaspoon salt
1³/₄ cups (11.5-ounce package) NESTLÉ® TOLL HOUSE® Milk
      Chocolate Morsels

PREHEAT oven to 375°F. Line baking sheets with foil.

MELT butter in medium saucepan; remove from heat. Stir in oats, sugar, flour, corn syrup, milk, vanilla extract and salt; mix well. Drop by level teaspoon, about 3 inches apart, onto prepared baking sheets. Spread thinly with rubber spatula.

BAKE for 6 to 8 minutes or until golden brown. Cool completely on baking sheets on wire racks. Peel foil from cookies.

MICROWAVE morsels in medium, uncovered microwave-safe bowl on MEDIUM-HIGH (70%) power for 1 minute. Stir. Morsels may retain some of their original shape. If necessary, microwave an additional 10- to 15-second intervals, stirring just until morsels are melted. Spread thin layer of melted chocolate onto flat side of *half* the cookies. Top with *remaining* cookies.   *Makes about 3¹/₂ dozen sandwich cookies*

best bet
bars

cranberry-lime squares

2¼ cups all-purpose flour, divided
½ cup powdered sugar
1 tablespoon plus 1 teaspoon grated lime peel
¼ teaspoon salt
1 cup (2 sticks) unsalted butter
4 eggs
2 cups granulated sugar
1 teaspoon baking powder
¼ cup lime juice (about 1½ limes)
1 cup dried cranberries
Additional powdered sugar

1. Preheat oven to 350°F. Grease 13×9-inch baking pan. Combine 2 cups flour, powdered sugar, 1 tablespoon lime peel and salt in medium bowl. Cut in butter with pastry blender or two knives until mixture forms coarse crumbs. Press mixture evenly into baking pan. Bake 18 to 20 minutes or until golden brown.

2. Meanwhile, combine remaining ¼ cup flour, granulated sugar and baking powder. In separate bowl, combine eggs and lime juice. Add flour mixture to egg mixture beating well on medium speed of electric mixer. Stir in remaining lime zest and cranberries. Pour over warm crust; bake 20 to 25 minutes until golden brown and set. Cool completely on wire rack. Sprinkle with powdered sugar; chill for two hours. Cut into squares. Serve chilled. *Makes 35 squares*

chocolatey raspberry crumb bars

1 cup (2 sticks) butter or margarine, softened
2 cups all-purpose flour
$^1/_2$ cup packed light brown sugar
$^1/_4$ teaspoon salt
2 cups (12-ounce package) NESTLÉ® TOLL HOUSE® Semi-Sweet
    Chocolate Morsels, *divided*
1 can (14 ounces) NESTLÉ® CARNATION® Sweetened Condensed
    Milk
$^1/_2$ cup chopped nuts (optional)
$^1/_3$ cup seedless raspberry jam

PREHEAT oven to 350°F. Grease 13×9-inch baking pan.

BEAT butter in large mixer bowl until creamy. Beat in flour, sugar and salt until crumbly. With floured fingers, press *1$^3/_4$ cups* crumb mixture onto bottom of prepared baking pan; reserve *remaining* mixture.

BAKE for 10 to 12 minutes or until edges are golden brown.

MICROWAVE *1 cup* morsels and sweetened condensed milk in medium, uncovered, microwave-safe bowl on HIGH (100%) power for 1 minute. STIR. Morsels may retain some of their original shape. If necessary, microwave at additional 10- to 15-second intervals, stirring just until morsels are melted. Spread over hot crust.

STIR nuts into *reserved* crumb mixture; sprinkle over chocolate layer. Drop teaspoonfuls of raspberry jam over crumb mixture. Sprinkle with *remaining* morsels.

BAKE for 25 to 30 minutes or until center is set. Cool in pan on wire rack. Cut into bars. *Makes 3 dozen bars*

magic cookie bars

½ cup (1 stick) butter or margarine
1½ cups graham cracker crumbs
1 (14-ounce) can EAGLE BRAND® Sweetened Condensed Milk
    (NOT evaporated milk)
2 cups (12 ounces) semi-sweet chocolate chips
1⅓ cups flaked coconut
1 cup chopped nuts

1. Preheat oven to 350°F (325°F for glass dish). In 13×9-inch baking pan, melt butter in oven.

2. Sprinkle crumbs over butter; pour Eagle Brand evenly over crumbs. Layer evenly with remaining ingredients; press down firmly.

3. Bake 25 minutes or until lightly browned. Cool. Chill, if desired. Cut into bars. Store loosely covered at room temperature.

Makes 2 to 3 dozen bars

7-layer magic cookie bars: Substitute 1 cup (6 ounces) butterscotch-flavored chips for 1 cup semi-sweet chocolate chips. (Peanut butter-flavored chips or white chocolate chips can be substituted for butterscotch-flavored chips.)

magic peanut cookie bars: Substitute 2 cups (about ¾ pound) chocolate-covered peanuts for semi-sweet chocolate chips and chopped nuts.

magic rainbow cookie bars: Substitute 2 cups plain candy-coated chocolate pieces for semi-sweet chocolate chips.

Prep Time: 10 minutes
Bake Time: 25 minutes

pumpkin harvest bars

1¾ cups all-purpose flour
2 teaspoons baking powder
1 teaspoon grated orange peel
1 teaspoon ground cinnamon
½ teaspoon salt
½ teaspoon ground nutmeg
¼ teaspoon ground ginger
¼ teaspoon ground cloves
¾ cup sugar
½ cup MOTT'S® Natural Apple Sauce
½ cup solid-pack pumpkin
1 whole egg
1 egg white
2 tablespoons vegetable oil
½ cup raisins

1. Preheat oven to 350°F. Spray 13×9-inch baking pan with nonstick cooking spray.

2. In small bowl, combine flour, baking powder, orange peel, cinnamon, salt, nutmeg, ginger and cloves.

3. In large bowl, combine sugar, apple sauce, pumpkin, whole egg, egg white and oil.

4. Add flour mixture to apple sauce mixture; stir until well blended. Stir in raisins. Spread batter into prepared pan.

5. Bake 25 to 30 minutes or until toothpick inserted in center comes out clean. Cool on wire rack 15 minutes; cut into 16 bars.

Makes 16 servings

almond fudge topped shortbread

    1 cup (2 sticks) butter or margarine, softened
    ½ cup powdered sugar
    ¼ teaspoon salt
    1¼ cups all-purpose flour
    2 cups (12-ounce package) HERSHEY₀S Semi-Sweet Chocolate
        Chips
    1 (14-ounce) can sweetened condensed milk (not evaporated
        milk)
    ½ teaspoon almond extract
    ½ cup sliced almonds, toasted

1. Heat oven to 350°F. Grease 13×9×2-inch baking pan.

2. Beat butter, powdered sugar and salt in large bowl until fluffy. Add flour; mix well. With floured hands, press evenly into prepared pan.

3. Bake 20 minutes or until lightly browned.

4. Melt chocolate chips and sweetened condensed milk in heavy saucepan over low heat, stirring constantly. Remove from heat; stir in extract. Spread evenly over baked shortbread. Garnish with almonds; press down firmly. Cool. Chill 3 hours or until firm. Cut into bars. Store covered at room temperature.   *Makes 24 to 36 bars*

candy bar bars

    ¾ cup (1½ sticks) butter or margarine, softened
    ¼ cup peanut butter
    1 cup firmly packed light brown sugar
    1 teaspoon baking soda
    2 cups quick-cooking oats
    1½ cups all-purpose flour
    1 egg
    1 (14-ounce) can EAGLE BRAND® Sweetened Condensed Milk
        (NOT evaporated milk)
    4 cups chopped candy bars (such as chocolate-coated caramel-
        topped nougat bars with peanuts, chocolate-covered crisp
        wafers, chocolate-covered caramel-topped cookie bars, or
        chocolate-covered peanut butter cups)

1. Preheat oven to 350°F. In large mixing bowl, combine butter and peanut butter. Add brown sugar and baking soda; beat well. Stir in oats and flour. Reserve 1¾ cups crumb mixture.

2. Stir egg into remaining crumb mixture; press firmly on bottom of ungreased 15×10×1-inch baking pan. Bake 15 minutes.

3. Pour Eagle Brand evenly over baked crust. Stir together reserved crumb mixture and candy bar pieces; sprinkle evenly over top. Bake 25 minutes or until golden. Cool. Cut into bars. Store covered at room temperature. *Makes 4 dozen bars*

Prep Time: 20 minutes
Bake Time: 40 minutes

hikers' bar cookies

- ³/₁ cup all-purpose flour
- ¹/₂ cup packed brown sugar
- ¹/₂ cup uncooked quick oats
- ¹/₄ cup toasted wheat germ
- ¹/₄ cup unsweetened applesauce
- ¹/₄ cup margarine or butter, softened
- ¹/₈ teaspoon salt
- ¹/₂ cup cholesterol-free egg substitute
- ¹/₄ cup raisins
- ¹/₄ cup dried cranberries
- ¹/₄ cup sunflower kernels
- 1 tablespoon grated orange peel
- 1 teaspoon ground cinnamon

1. Preheat oven to 350°F. Lightly coat 13×9-inch baking pan with nonstick cooking spray; set aside.

2. Beat flour, sugar, oats, wheat germ, applesauce, margarine and salt in large bowl with electric mixer at medium speed until well blended. Add egg substitute, raisins, cranberries, sunflower kernels, orange peel and cinnamon. Spread into pan.

3. Bake 15 minutes or until firm to touch. Cool completely in pan. Cut into 24 squares. *Makes 24 servings*

swirled peanut butter chocolate cheesecake bars

Crust

> 2 cups graham cracker crumbs
> ½ cup (1 stick) butter or margarine, melted
> ⅓ cup granulated sugar

Filling

> 2 packages (8 ounces *each*) cream cheese, softened
> 1 cup granulated sugar
> ¼ cup all-purpose flour
> 1 can (12 fluid ounces) NESTLÉ® CARNATION® Evaporated Milk
> 2 large eggs
> 1 tablespoon vanilla extract
> 1 cup (6 ounces) NESTLÉ® TOLL HOUSE® Peanut Butter & Milk Chocolate Morsels

PREHEAT oven to 325°F.

For Crust

COMBINE graham cracker crumbs, butter and sugar in medium bowl; press onto bottom of ungreased 13×9-inch baking pan.

For Filling

BEAT cream cheese, sugar and flour in large mixer bowl until smooth. Gradually beat in evaporated milk, eggs and vanilla extract.

MICROWAVE morsels in medium, uncovered, microwave-safe bowl on MEDIUM-HIGH (70%) power for 1 minute. STIR. Morsels may retain some of their original shape. If necessary, microwave at additional 10- to 15-second intervals, stirring just until morsels are melted. Stir *1 cup* cream cheese mixture into chocolate. Pour *remaining* cream cheese mixture over crust. Pour chocolate mixture over cream cheese mixture. Swirl mixtures with spoon, pulling plain cream cheese mixture up to surface.

BAKE for 40 to 45 minutes or until set. Cool completely in pan on wire rack; refrigerate until firm. Cut into bars.   *Makes 15 bars*

oatmeal toffee bars

1 cup (2 sticks) butter or margarine, softened
$^1/_2$ cup packed light brown sugar
$^1/_2$ cup granulated sugar
2 eggs
1 teaspoon vanilla extract
$1^1/_2$ cups all-purpose flour
1 teaspoon baking soda
$^1/_2$ teaspoon ground cinnamon
$^1/_2$ teaspoon salt
3 cups quick-cooking or regular rolled oats
$1^3/_4$ cups (10-ounce package) SKOR® English Toffee Bits or
$1^3/_4$ cups HEATH® BITS 'O BRICKLE™, divided

1. Heat oven to 350°F. Grease 13×9×2-inch baking pan.

2. Beat butter, brown sugar and granulated sugar in large bowl until well blended. Add eggs and vanilla; beat well. Stir together flour, baking soda, cinnamon and salt; gradually add to butter mixture, beating until well blended. Stir in oats and $1^1/_3$ cups toffee bits (mixture will be stiff). Spread mixture into prepared pan.

3. Bake 25 minutes or until wooden pick inserted in center comes out clean. Immediately sprinkle remaining toffee bits over surface. Cool completely in pan on wire rack. Cut into bars.   *Makes about 36 bars*

tip: Bar cookies can be cut into different shapes for variety. To cut into triangles, cut cookie bars into 2- to 3-inch squares, then diagonally cut each square in half. To make diamond shapes, cut parallel lines 2 inches apart across the length of the pan, then cut diagonal lines 2 inches apart.

almond chinese chews

1 cup granulated sugar
3 eggs, lightly beaten
1 can SOLO® or 1 jar BAKER® Almond Filling
¾ cup all-purpose flour
1 teaspoon baking powder
¼ teaspoon salt
  Powdered sugar

Preheat oven to 300°F. Grease 13×9-inch baking pan; set aside.

Beat granulated sugar and eggs in medium-size bowl with electric mixer until thoroughly blended. Add almond filling; beat until blended. Sift together flour, baking powder and salt; fold into almond mixture. Spread batter evenly in prepared pan.

Bake 40 to 45 minutes or until wooden toothpick inserted in center comes out clean. Cool completely in pan on wire rack. Cut into 2×1½-inch bars; dust with powdered sugar.

Makes about 3 dozen bars

For easy removal of brownies and bar cookies (and no cleanup!), line the baking pan with foil and leave at least 3 inches hanging over each end. Use the foil to lift out the treats, place them on a cutting board and carefully remove the foil. Then simply cut them into pieces.

coconut almond bars

Crust

    1½ cups all-purpose flour
    1 cup butter, softened
    ½ cup sugar
    ½ cup ground almonds
    ½ teaspoon almond extract

Filling

    1 cup sugar
    1 egg
    2 tablespoons all-purpose flour
    2 teaspoons vanilla
    ½ teaspoon baking powder
    ½ teaspoon salt
    1 cup flaked coconut
    ¾ cup lightly toasted slivered almonds, divided
    2 teaspoons milk

Crust

Preheat oven to 350°F. Combine all crust ingredients in small bowl.
Beat at low speed of electric mixer, scraping bowl often, until particles
are fine, 2 to 3 minutes. Press on bottom of 13×9-inch baking pan.
Bake 15 to 20 minutes or until edges are lightly browned.

Filling

Combine sugar, egg, flour, vanilla, baking powder and salt in small
bowl. Beat at medium speed of electric mixer, scraping bowl often,
until well mixed, 1 to 2 minutes. Stir in coconut, ½ cup nuts and milk.
Pour over hot crust. Sprinkle top with remaining ¼ cup nuts. Bake an
additional 20 to 25 minutes or until lightly browned.

Makes about 36 bars

brownie caramel pecan bars

$^1/_2$ cup sugar
2 tablespoons butter or margarine
2 tablespoons water
2 cups (12-ounce package) HERSHEY'S Semi-Sweet Chocolate
   Chips, divided
2 eggs
1 teaspoon vanilla extract
$^2/_3$ cup all-purpose flour
$^1/_4$ teaspoon baking soda
$^1/_4$ teaspoon salt
   Classic Caramel Topping (recipe follows)
1 cup pecan pieces

1. Heat oven to 350°F. Line 9-inch square baking pan with foil, extending foil over edges of pan. Grease and flour foil.

2. Combine sugar, butter and water in medium saucepan. Cook over low heat, stirring constantly, until mixture boils. Remove from heat. Immediately add 1 cup chocolate chips; stir until melted. Beat in eggs and vanilla until well blended. Stir together flour, baking soda and salt; stir into chocolate mixture. Spread batter into prepared pan.

3. Bake 15 to 20 minutes or until brownies begin to pull away from sides of pan. Meanwhile, prepare Classic Caramel Topping. Remove brownies from oven; immediately and carefully spread with prepared topping. Sprinkle remaining 1 cup chips and pecans over topping. Cool completely in pan on wire rack, being careful not to disturb chips while soft. Lift out of pan. Cut into bars.

Makes about 16 bars

classic caramel topping: Remove wrappers from 25 HERSHEY'S Classic Caramels. Combine $^1/_4$ cup ($^1/_2$ stick) butter or margarine, caramels and 2 tablespoons milk in medium microwave-safe bowl. Microwave at HIGH (100%) 1 minute; stir. Microwave an additional 1 to 2 minutes, stirring every 30 seconds, or until caramels are melted and mixture is smooth when stirred. Use immediately.

razz-ma-tazz bars

 1/2 cup (1 stick) butter or margarine
 2 cups (12-ounce package) NESTLÉ® TOLL HOUSE® Premier
   White Morsels, *divided*
 2 large eggs
 1/2 cup granulated sugar
 1 cup all-purpose flour
 1/2 teaspoon salt
 1/2 teaspoon almond extract
 1/2 cup seedless raspberry jam
 1/4 cup toasted sliced almonds

PREHEAT oven to 325°F. Grease and sugar 9-inch square baking pan.

MELT butter in medium, microwave-safe bowl on HIGH (100%) power for 1 minute; stir. Add *1 cup* morsels; let stand. Do not stir.

BEAT eggs in large mixer bowl until foamy. Add sugar; beat until light lemon colored, about 5 minutes. Stir in morsel-butter mixture. Add flour, salt and almond extract; mix at low speed until combined. Spread 2/3 of batter into prepared pan.

BAKE for 15 to 17 minutes or until light golden brown around edges. Remove from oven to wire rack.

HEAT jam in small, microwave-safe bowl on HIGH (100%) power for 30 seconds; stir. Spread jam over warm crust. Stir *remaining* morsels into *remaining* batter. Drop spoonfuls of batter over jam. Sprinkle with almonds.

BAKE for 25 to 30 minutes or until edges are browned. Cool completely in pan on wire rack. Cut into bars. *Makes 16 bars*

dulce de leche blondies

        2 cups all-purpose flour
        1 teaspoon baking soda
        1 teaspoon salt
        1 cup (2 sticks) unsalted butter, softened
        1 cup firmly packed brown sugar
        2 eggs
    1½ teaspoons vanilla
        1 (14-ounce) package caramels
      ½ cup evaporated milk

1. Preheat oven to 350°F. Grease 13×9-inch baking pan. Sift together flour, soda and salt in medium bowl; set aside.

2. Beat butter and sugar in large bowl with electric mixer on medium speed until creamy. Add eggs and vanilla; beat until smooth. Gradually stir in flour mixture. Spread ½ to ⅔ of mixture in pan. Bake 7 to 8 minutes. Let cool 5 minutes on wire rack.

3. Meanwhile, melt caramels in evaporated milk in nonstick saucepan over very low heat. Reserve 2 tablespoons. Pour remaining caramel over bottom layer. Drop dollops of remaining dough over caramel layer; swirl slightly with knife.

4. Bake 25 minutes or until golden brown. Cool in pan on wire rack. When completely cooled, cut into squares. Drizzle with reserved caramel, heating as necessary.   *Makes about 3 dozen blondies*

rocky road bars

2 cups (12-ounce package) NESTLÉ® TOLL HOUSE® Semi-Sweet
    Chocolate Morsels, *divided*
1¹/₂ cups all-purpose flour
1¹/₂ teaspoons baking powder
  1 cup granulated sugar
  6 tablespoons (³/₄ stick) butter or margarine, softened
1¹/₂ teaspoons vanilla extract
  2 large eggs
  2 cups miniature marshmallows
1¹/₂ cups coarsely chopped walnuts

PREHEAT oven to 375°F. Grease 13×9-inch baking pan.

MICROWAVE *1 cup* morsels in medium, uncovered, microwave-safe
bowl on HIGH (100%) power for 1 minute. STIR. Morsels may retain
some of their original shape. If necessary, microwave at additional
10- to 15-second intervals, stirring just until morsels are melted. Cool
to room temperature. Combine flour and baking powder in small bowl.

BEAT sugar, butter and vanilla in large mixer bowl until crumbly. Beat
in eggs. Add melted chocolate; beat until smooth. Gradually beat in
flour mixture. Spread batter into prepared baking pan.

BAKE for 16 to 20 minutes or until wooden pick inserted in center
comes out slightly sticky.

REMOVE from oven; sprinkle immediately with marshmallows, nuts
and *remaining* morsels. Return to oven for 2 minutes or just until
marshmallows begin to melt. Cool in pan on wire rack for 20 to
30 minutes. Cut into bars with wet knife. Serve warm.

Makes 2¹/₂ dozen bars

fruit and nut bars

1 cup unsifted all-purpose flour
1 cup quick oats
²/₃ cup brown sugar
2 teaspoons baking soda
½ teaspoon salt
½ teaspoon cinnamon
²/₃ cup buttermilk
3 tablespoons vegetable oil
2 egg whites, lightly beaten
1 Washington Golden Delicious apple, cored and chopped
½ cup dried cranberries or raisins, chopped
¼ cup chopped nuts
2 tablespoons flaked coconut (optional)

1. Heat oven to 375°F. Lightly grease 9-inch square baking pan. In large mixing bowl, combine flour, oats, brown sugar, baking soda, salt and cinnamon; stir to blend.

2. Add buttermilk, oil and egg whites; beat with electric mixer just until mixed. Stir in apple, dried fruit and nuts; spread evenly in pan and top with coconut, if desired. Bake 20 to 25 minutes or until cake tester inserted in center comes out clean. Cool and cut into 10 bars.

Makes 10 bars

Favorite recipe from **Washington Apple Commission**

ultimate
brownies

fudgy hazelnut brownies

1 (21-ounce) package DUNCAN HINES® Chewy
    Fudge Brownie Mix
2 eggs
½ cup vegetable oil
¼ cup water
1 cup chopped toasted hazelnuts
1 cup semisweet chocolate chips
1 cup DUNCAN HINES® Dark Chocolate Frosting
3 squares white chocolate, melted

1. Preheat oven to 350°F. Grease bottom only of 13×9-inch baking pan.

2. Combine brownie mix, eggs, oil and water in large bowl. Stir with spoon until well blended, about 50 strokes. Stir in hazelnuts and chocolate chips. Spread in prepared pan. Bake at 350°F for 25 to 30 minutes or until set. Cool completely.

3. Heat frosting in microwave oven at HIGH for 15 seconds or until thin; stir well. Spread over brownies. Spoon dollops of white chocolate over chocolate frosting; marble white chocolate through frosting. Cool completely. Cut into bars.   *Makes 24 brownies*

Toasting nuts before using them intensifies their flavor and crunch. To toast nuts, spread them on a baking sheet and place in a 350°F oven for 8 to 10 minutes. Or, toast nuts in an ungreased skillet over medium heat until golden brown, stirring frequently. Always cool nuts to room temperature before combining them with other ingredients.

cheesecake-topped brownies

1 (21.5- or 23.6-ounce) package fudge brownie mix
1 (8-ounce) package cream cheese, softened
2 tablespoons butter or margarine, softened
1 tablespoon cornstarch
1 (14-ounce) can EAGLE BRAND® Sweetened Condensed Milk
   (NOT evaporated milk)
1 egg
2 teaspoons vanilla extract
  Ready-to-spread chocolate frosting, if desired
  Orange peel, if desired

1. Preheat oven to 350°F. Prepare brownie mix as package directs. Spread into well-greased 13×9-inch baking pan.

2. In large mixing bowl, beat cream cheese, butter and cornstarch until fluffy.

3. Gradually beat in Eagle Brand. Add egg and vanilla; beat until smooth. Pour cheesecake mixture evenly over brownie batter.

4. Bake 40 to 45 minutes or until top is lightly browned. Cool. Spread with frosting or sprinkle with orange peel, if desired. Cut into bars. Store covered in refrigerator. *Makes 3 to 3¹/₂ dozen brownies*

Prep Time: 20 minutes
Bake Time: 40 to 45 minutes

orange cappuccino brownies

¾ cup (1½ sticks) butter
2 squares (1 ounce each) semisweet chocolate, coarsely chopped
2 squares (1 ounce each) unsweetened chocolate, coarsely chopped
1¾ cups granulated sugar
1 tablespoon instant espresso powder or instant coffee granules
3 eggs
¼ cup orange-flavored liqueur
2 teaspoons grated orange peel
1 cup all-purpose flour
1 package (12 ounces) semisweet chocolate chips
2 tablespoons shortening

Preheat oven to 350°F. Grease 13×9-inch baking pan.

Melt butter and semisweet and unsweetened chocolate in large heavy saucepan over low heat, stirring constantly. Stir in granulated sugar and espresso powder. Remove from heat. Cool slightly. Beat in eggs, 1 at a time. Whisk in liqueur and orange peel. Beat flour into chocolate mixture just until blended. Spread batter evenly in prepared pan.

Bake 25 to 30 minutes or until center is just set. Remove pan to wire rack. Meanwhile, melt chocolate chips and shortening in small heavy saucepan over low heat, stirring constantly. Immediately spread hot chocolate mixture over warm brownies. Cool completely in pan on wire rack. Cut into 2-inch squares.   *Makes about 2 dozen brownies*

chocolate marbled blondies

$^1\!/_2$ **cup (1 stick) butter or margarine, softened**
$^1\!/_2$ **cup firmly packed light brown sugar**
1 **large egg**
2 **teaspoons vanilla extract**
1$^1\!/_2$ **cups all-purpose flour**
1$^1\!/_4$ **teaspoons baking soda**
1 **cup "M&M's"® Chocolate Mini Baking Bits, divided**
4 **ounces cream cheese, softened**
2 **tablespoons granulated sugar**
1 **large egg yolk**
$^1\!/_4$ **cup unsweetened cocoa powder**

Preheat oven to 350°F. Lightly grease 9×9×2-inch baking pan; set aside. In large bowl cream butter and brown sugar until light and fluffy; beat in egg and vanilla. In medium bowl combine flour and baking soda; blend into creamed mixture. Stir in $^2\!/_3$ cup "M&M's"® Chocolate Mini Baking Bits; set aside. Dough will be stiff. In separate bowl beat together cream cheese, granulated sugar and egg yolk until smooth; stir in cocoa powder until well blended. Place chocolate-cheese mixture in six equal portions evenly onto bottom of prepared pan. Place reserved dough around cheese mixture and swirl slightly with tines of fork. Pat down evenly on top. Sprinkle with remaining $^1\!/_3$ cup "M&M's"® Chocolate Mini Baking Bits. Bake 25 to 30 minutes or until toothpick inserted in center comes out with moist crumbs. Cool completely. Cut into bars. Store in refrigerator in tightly covered container. *Makes 16 bars*

fudgy brownie bars

    1 package (about 20 ounces) brownie mix
    2 eggs
    $^{1}/_{3}$ cup water
    $^{1}/_{3}$ cup vegetable oil
    1 (6-ounce) package semisweet chocolate chips
    $^{2}/_{3}$ cup butterscotch chips
    $^{2}/_{3}$ cup chopped pecans
    $^{3}/_{4}$ cup flaked coconut
    1 (14-ounce) can sweetened condensed milk

Preheat oven to 350°F. Grease 13×9-inch pan.

Combine brownie mix, eggs, water and oil in large bowl. Stir with spoon until well blended, about 50 strokes. Spread into prepared pan. Bake 18 minutes. Remove from oven. Sprinkle chocolate chips over brownie base; layer butterscotch chips, pecans and coconut over chocolate chips. Pour condensed milk over top. Bake 22 to 25 minutes or until light golden brown. Cool completely in pan on wire rack. Cut into bars.   *Makes 24 bars*

tip: Peanut butter chips may be substituted for the butterscotch chips.

miniature brownie cups

6 tablespoons butter or margarine, melted
$^3/_4$ cup sugar
$^1/_2$ teaspoon vanilla extract
2 eggs
$^1/_2$ cup all-purpose flour
$^1/_4$ cup HERSHEY'S Cocoa or HERSHEY'S Dutch Processed Cocoa
$^1/_4$ teaspoon baking powder
   Dash salt
$^1/_4$ cup finely chopped nuts

1. Heat oven to 350°F. Line small muffin cups ($1^3/_4$ inches in diameter) with paper bake cups. Stir together butter, sugar and vanilla in medium bowl. Add eggs; beat well with spoon.

2. Stir together flour, cocoa, baking powder and salt; gradually add to butter mixture, beating with spoon until well blended. Fill muffin cups $^1/_2$ full with batter; sprinkle nuts over top.

3. Bake 12 to 15 minutes or until wooden pick inserted in center comes out almost clean. Cool slightly; remove brownies from pan to wire rack. Cool completely.   *Makes about 24 brownies*

tip: HERSHEY'S Dutch Processed Cocoa involves a process which neutralizes the natural acidity found in cocoa powder. This results in a darker cocoa with a more mellow flavor than natural cocoa.

Prep Time: 20 minutes
Bake Time: 12 minutes
Cool Time: 25 minutes

cheery cherry brownies

¾ cup all-purpose flour
½ cup sugar substitute
½ cup unsweetened cocoa powder
¼ teaspoon baking soda
½ cup evaporated skimmed milk
⅓ cup butter, melted
¼ cup cholesterol-free egg substitute
¼ cup honey
1 teaspoon vanilla
½ (15½-ounce) can pitted tart red cherries, drained and halved

1. Preheat oven to 350°F. Grease 11×7-inch baking pan; set aside.

2. Stir together flour, sweetener, cocoa powder and baking soda in large mixing bowl. Add milk, butter, egg substitute, honey and vanilla. Stir just until mixed.

3. Pour into prepared pan. Sprinkle cherries over top of chocolate mixture. Bake 13 to 15 minutes or until toothpick inserted into center comes out clean. Cool. Cut into 12 equal-size brownies.

Makes 12 servings

bamboozlers

1 cup all-purpose flour
¾ cup packed light brown sugar
¼ cup unsweetened cocoa powder
1 egg
2 egg whites
5 tablespoons margarine, melted
¼ cup fat-free (skim) milk
¼ cup honey
1 teaspoon vanilla
2 tablespoons semisweet chocolate chips
2 tablespoons coarsely chopped walnuts
Powdered sugar (optional)

1. Preheat oven to 350°F. Grease and flour 8-inch square baking pan; set aside.

2. Combine flour, brown sugar and cocoa in medium bowl. Blend together egg, egg whites, margarine, milk, honey and vanilla in medium bowl. Add to flour mixture; mix well. Pour into prepared baking pan; sprinkle with chocolate chips and walnuts.

3. Bake brownies until they spring back when lightly touched in center, about 30 minutes. Cool completely in pan on wire rack. Sprinkle with powdered sugar just before serving, if desired.

Makes 1 dozen brownies

peanutters: Substitute peanut butter chips for chocolate chips and peanuts for walnuts.

butterscotch babies: Substitute butterscotch chips for chocolate chips and pecans for walnuts.

brownie sundaes: Serve brownies on dessert plates. Top each brownie with a scoop of vanilla nonfat frozen yogurt and 2 tablespoons nonfat chocolate or caramel sauce.

marbled peanut butter brownies

   $\frac{1}{2}$ cup butter, softened
   $\frac{1}{4}$ cup peanut butter
    1 cup packed light brown sugar
   $\frac{1}{2}$ cup granulated sugar
    3 eggs
    1 teaspoon vanilla
    2 cups all-purpose flour
    2 teaspoons baking powder
   $\frac{1}{8}$ teaspoon salt
    1 cup chocolate syrup
   $\frac{1}{2}$ cup coarsely chopped salted mixed nuts

Preheat oven to 350°F. Lightly grease 13×9-inch pan. Beat butter and peanut butter in large bowl until blended; stir in sugars. Beat in eggs, one at a time, until well blended. Blend in vanilla. Combine flour, baking powder and salt in small bowl. Stir into butter mixture. Spread half of batter evenly in prepared pan. Spread syrup over top. Spoon remaining batter over syrup. Swirl with knife or spatula to create marbled effect. Sprinkle with chopped nuts. Bake 35 to 40 minutes or until lightly browned. Cool in pan on wire rack. Cut into 2-inch squares. *Makes about 2 dozen brownies*

fudge topped brownies

    2 cups sugar
    1 cup (2 sticks) butter or margarine, melted
    1 cup all-purpose flour
   $\frac{2}{3}$ cup unsweetened cocoa
   $\frac{1}{2}$ teaspoon baking powder
    2 eggs
   $\frac{1}{2}$ cup milk
    3 teaspoons vanilla extract, divided
    1 cup chopped nuts, if desired
    2 cups (12 ounces) semi-sweet chocolate chips
    1 (14-ounce) can EAGLE BRAND® Sweetened Condensed Milk
       (NOT evaporated milk)
    Dash salt

1. Preheat oven to 350°F. In large mixing bowl, combine sugar, butter, flour, cocoa, baking powder, eggs, milk and 1½ teaspoons vanilla; mix well. Stir in nuts, if desired. Spread in greased 13×9-inch baking pan. Bake 40 minutes or until brownies begin to pull away from sides of pan.

2. Meanwhile, in heavy saucepan over low heat, melt chips with Eagle Brand, remaining 1½ teaspoons vanilla and salt. Remove from heat. Immediately spread over hot brownies. Cool. Chill. Cut into bars. Store covered at room temperature. *Makes 3 to 3½ dozen brownies*

minted chocolate chip brownies

  ¾ **cup granulated sugar**
  ½ **cup butter**
  2 **tablespoons water**
  1 **cup semisweet chocolate chips or mini semisweet chocolate chips**
  1½ **teaspoons vanilla**
  2 **eggs**
  1¼ **cups all-purpose flour**
  ½ **teaspoon baking soda**
  ½ **teaspoon salt**
  1 **cup mint chocolate chips**
    Powdered sugar for garnish

Preheat oven to 350°F. Grease 9-inch square baking pan. Combine sugar, butter and water in medium microwavable bowl. Microwave at HIGH 2½ to 3 minutes or until butter is melted. Stir in semisweet chips; stir gently until chips are melted and mixture is well blended. Stir in vanilla; let stand 5 minutes to cool.

Beat eggs into chocolate mixture, one at a time. Combine flour, baking soda and salt in small bowl; add to chocolate mixture. Stir in mint chocolate chips. Spread in prepared pan.

Bake 25 minutes for fudgy brownies or 30 minutes for cakelike brownies.

Remove pan to wire rack; cool completely. Cut into 2¼-inch squares. Sprinkle with powdered sugar, if desired. *Makes about 16 brownies*

coconutty "m&m's"® brownies

6 squares (1 ounce each) semi-sweet chocolate
$^3/_4$ cup granulated sugar
$^1/_2$ cup (1 stick) butter
2 large eggs
1 tablespoon vegetable oil
1 teaspoon vanilla extract
$1^1/_4$ cups all-purpose flour
3 tablespoons unsweetened cocoa powder
1 teaspoon baking powder
$^1/_2$ teaspoon salt
$1^1/_2$ cups "M&M's"® Chocolate Mini Baking Bits, divided
Coconut Topping (recipe follows)

Preheat oven to 350°F. Lightly grease 8×8×2-inch baking pan; set aside. In small saucepan combine chocolate, sugar and butter over low heat; stir constantly until chocolate is melted. Remove from heat; let cool slightly. In large bowl beat eggs, oil and vanilla; stir in chocolate mixture until well blended. In medium bowl combine flour, cocoa powder, baking powder and salt; add to chocolate mixture. Stir in 1 cup "M&M's"® Chocolate Mini Baking Bits. Spread batter evenly in prepared pan. Bake 35 to 40 minutes or until toothpick inserted in center comes out clean. Cool completely on wire rack. Prepare Coconut Topping. Spread over brownies; sprinkle with remaining $^1/_2$ cup "M&M's"® Chocolate Mini Baking Bits. Cut into bars. Store in tightly covered container.   *Makes 16 brownies*

coconut topping

$^1/_2$ cup (1 stick) butter
$^1/_3$ cup firmly packed light brown sugar
$^1/_3$ cup light corn syrup
1 cup sweetened shredded coconut, toasted*
$^3/_4$ cup chopped pecans
1 teaspoon vanilla extract

To toast coconut, spread evenly on cookie sheet. Toast in preheated 350°F oven 7 to 8 minutes or until golden brown, stirring occasionally.

In large saucepan melt butter over medium heat; add brown sugar and corn syrup, stirring constantly until thick and bubbly. Remove from heat and stir in remaining ingredients.

bittersweet pecan brownies with caramel sauce

BROWNIES
- ³/₄ cup all-purpose flour
- ¹/₄ teaspoon baking soda
- 4 squares (1 ounce each) bittersweet or unsweetened chocolate, coarsely chopped
- ¹/₂ cup (1 stick) plus 2 tablespoons I CAN'T BELIEVE IT'S NOT BUTTER!® Spread
- ³/₄ cup sugar
- 2 eggs
- ¹/₂ cup chopped pecans

CARAMEL SAUCE
- ³/₄ cup firmly packed light brown sugar
- 6 tablespoons I CAN'T BELIEVE IT'S NOT BUTTER!® Spread
- ¹/₃ cup whipping or heavy cream
- ¹/₂ teaspoon apple cider vinegar or fresh lemon juice

For brownies, preheat oven to 325°F. Line 8-inch square baking pan with aluminum foil, then grease and flour foil; set aside.

In small bowl, combine flour and baking soda; set aside.

In medium microwave-safe bowl, microwave chocolate and I Can't Believe It's Not Butter!® Spread at HIGH (Full Power) 1 minute or until chocolate is melted; stir until smooth. With wooden spoon, beat in sugar, then eggs. Beat in flour mixture. Evenly spread into prepared pan; sprinkle with pecans.

Bake 31 minutes or until toothpick inserted in center comes out clean. On wire rack, cool completely. To remove brownies, lift edges of foil. Cut brownies into 4 squares, then cut each square into 2 triangles.

For caramel sauce, in medium saucepan, bring brown sugar, I Can't Believe It's Not Butter! Spread and cream just to a boil over high heat, stirring frequently. Cook 3 minutes. Stir in vinegar. To serve, pour caramel sauce around brownie and top, if desired, with vanilla or caramel ice cream. *Makes 8 servings*

double mint brownies

1 (21-ounce) package DUNCAN HINES® Family-Style Chewy
   Recipe Fudge Brownie Mix
1 egg
$^1/_3$ cup water
$^1/_3$ cup vegetable oil plus additional for greasing
$^1/_2$ teaspoon peppermint extract
24 chocolate-covered peppermint patties ($1^1/_2$ inches each)
1 cup confectioners' sugar, divided
4 teaspoons milk, divided
   Red food coloring
   Green food coloring

1. Preheat oven to 350°F. Grease bottom only of 13×9×2-inch pan. Combine brownie mix, egg, water, oil and peppermint extract in large bowl. Stir with spoon until well blended, about 50 strokes. Spread in prepared pan. Bake brownies following package directions. Place peppermint patties on warm brownies. Cool completely.

2. Combine $^1/_2$ cup confectioners' sugar, 2 teaspoons milk and 1 drop red food coloring in small bowl. Stir until smooth. Place in small resealable plastic bag; set aside. Repeat with remaining $^1/_2$ cup confectioners' sugar, remaining 2 teaspoons milk and 1 drop green food coloring. Cut pinpoint hole in bottom corner of each bag. Drizzle pink and green glazes over brownies as shown. Allow glazes to set before cutting into bars. *Makes 24 brownies*

tip: To prevent overdone edges and underdone center, wrap foil strips around outside edges of pan (do not cover bottom or top). Bake as directed above.

cream cheese brownie royale

  1 package (about 15 ounces) low-fat brownie mix
²/₃ cup cold coffee or water
  1 package (8 ounces) reduced-fat cream cheese, softened
¼ cup fat-free (skim) milk
  5 packets sugar substitute *or* equivalent of 10 teaspoons sugar
½ teaspoon vanilla

1. Preheat oven to 350°F. Coat 13×9-inch nonstick baking pan with nonstick cooking spray.

2. Combine brownie mix and coffee in large bowl; stir until blended. Pour brownie mixture into prepared pan.

3. Beat cream cheese, milk, sugar substitute and vanilla in medium bowl with electric mixer at medium speed until smooth. Spoon cream cheese mixture in dollops over brownie mixture. Swirl cream cheese mixture into brownie mixture with tip of knife.

4. Bake 30 to 35 minutes or until toothpick inserted in center comes out clean. Cool completely in pan on wire rack.

5. Cover with foil and refrigerate 8 hours or until ready to serve. Garnish as desired.   *Makes 16 servings*

nutty
for nuts

chocolate macadamia crunch

1 Butter Flavor CRISCO® Stick or 1 cup Butter Flavor CRISCO®
  all-vegetable shortening plus additional for greasing
$^3/_4$ cup granulated sugar
$^1/_2$ cup firmly packed dark brown sugar
2 eggs
2 tablespoons buttermilk
2 teaspoons vanilla
$1^1/_2$ cups all-purpose flour
$^1/_2$ cup oats (old-fashioned, uncooked)
1 teaspoon baking soda
$^1/_2$ teaspoon salt
2 cups milk chocolate chips
1 cup coarsely chopped macadamia nuts

1. Combine shortening, granulated sugar, brown sugar, eggs, buttermilk and vanilla in large bowl. Beat at medium speed of electric mixer until light and fluffy.

2. Combine flour, oats, baking soda and salt. Add gradually to creamed mixture at low speed. Beat until well blended. Stir in chocolate chips and nuts with spoon. Cover. Refrigerate at least 30 minutes.

3. Heat oven to 325°F. Grease baking sheet with shortening. Place sheets of foil on countertop for cooling cookies.

4. Drop dough by tablespoonfuls 3 inches apart onto greased baking sheet.

5. Bake at 325°F for 14 to 16 minutes or until light golden brown. *Do not overbake.* Cool 2 minutes on baking sheet. Remove cookies to foil to cool completely.   *Makes about $2^1/_2$ dozen cookies*

ultimate rocky road cups

  ¾ cup (1½ sticks) butter or margarine
  4 squares (1 ounce each) unsweetened baking chocolate
1½ cups granulated sugar
  3 large eggs
  1 cup all-purpose flour
1¾ cups "M&M's"® Chocolate Mini Baking Bits
  ¾ cup coarsely chopped peanuts
  1 cup mini marshmallows

Preheat oven to 350°F. Generously grease 24 (2½-inch) muffin cups
or line with foil liners. Place butter and chocolate in large microwave-
safe bowl. Microwave on HIGH 1 minute; stir. Microwave on HIGH an
additional 30 seconds; stir until chocolate is completely melted. Add
sugar and eggs, one at a time, beating well after each addition; blend
in flour. In separate bowl combine "M&M's"® Chocolate Mini Baking
Bits and nuts; stir 1 cup baking bits mixture into brownie batter.
Divide batter evenly among prepared muffin cups. Bake 20 minutes.
Combine remaining baking bits mixture with marshmallows; divide
evenly among muffin cups, topping hot brownies. Return to oven;
bake 5 minutes longer. Cool completely before removing from muffin
cups. Store in tightly covered container.   *Makes 24 cups*

mini ultimate rocky road cups: Prepare recipe as directed, dividing
batter among 60 generously greased 2-inch mini muffin cups. Bake
15 minutes. Sprinkle with topping mixture; bake 5 minutes longer.
Cool completely before removing from cups. Store in tightly covered
container. Makes about 60 mini cups.

ultimate rocky road squares: Prepare recipe as directed, spreading
batter into generously greased 13×9×2-inch baking pan. Bake
30 minutes. Sprinkle with topping mixture; bake 5 minutes longer.
Cool completely. Cut into squares. Store in tightly covered container.
Makes 24 squares.

quebec maple-pecan drops

Cookies
- ½ cup butter, softened
- ½ cup granulated sugar
- 3 tablespoons maple-flavored pancake syrup
- 1 cup all-purpose flour
- ½ teaspoon baking soda
- ¼ teaspoon salt
- 1 cup uncooked quick oats (not old-fashioned oats)
- ½ cup coarsely chopped pecans, toasted
- ¼ cup packaged chopped pitted dates

Frosting (optional)
- 2 ounces cream cheese, softened
- 2 tablespoons butter, softened
- 2 tablespoons maple flavored pancake syrup
- 1½ cups sifted powdered sugar
- ⅓ cup finely chopped pecans, toasted

1. Preheat oven to 350°F. Beat butter and granulated sugar in large bowl of electric mixer at medium speed until creamy. Beat in 3 tablespoons syrup. Combine flour, baking soda and salt; gradually beat into butter mixture. On low speed, beat in oats, coarsely chopped pecans and dates.

2. Drop dough by rounded tablespoonfuls 2 inches apart onto ungreased cookie sheets. Bake 12 minutes or until cookies are golden brown. Let stand on cookie sheets 2 minutes; transfer to wire racks and cool completely.

3. For frosting, if desired, beat cream cheese and butter in small bowl of electric mixer at medium speed until smooth. Beat in 2 tablespoons syrup. Gradually beat in powdered sugar until smooth. Spread frosting over cooled cookies; top with finely chopped pecans.

Makes about 2 dozen cookies

peanut butter crinkles

1 cup JIF® Crunchy Peanut Butter, divided
½ Butter Flavor CRISCO® Stick or ½ cup Butter Flavor CRISCO®
   all-vegetable shortening plus additional for greasing
½ cup granulated sugar
½ cup firmly packed light brown sugar
1 egg, well beaten
½ teaspoon vanilla
1⅓ cups all-purpose flour
¾ teaspoon baking soda
½ teaspoon baking powder
¼ teaspoon salt
⅔ cup confectioners' sugar
   Granulated sugar

1. Combine ½ cup peanut butter, shortening, granulated sugar and brown sugar in large bowl. Beat at medium speed of electric mixer until well blended. Beat in egg and vanilla.

2. Combine flour, baking soda, baking powder and salt. Add gradually to creamed mixture at low speed. Beat until well blended. Cover. Refrigerate 1 hour.

3. Combine remaining ½ cup peanut butter and confectioners' sugar in small bowl. Stir with fork until well blended (mixture will clump together and appear moist).

4. Heat oven to 350°F. Grease baking sheet with shortening. Place sheets of foil on countertop for cooling cookies.

5. Shape dough into 1¼-inch balls. Roll in peanut butter mixture (balls will not be evenly coated). Place 2 inches apart on prepared baking sheet. Flatten with bottom of glass dipped in granulated sugar.

6. Bake at 350°F for 8 to 10 minutes or until light brown and just set. *Do not overbake.* Cool on baking sheet. Remove cookies to foil to cool completely. *Makes about 3½ dozen cookies*

orange pecan gems →

1 package DUNCAN HINES® Moist Deluxe® Orange Supreme
   Cake Mix
1 container (8 ounces) vanilla low fat yogurt
1 egg
2 tablespoons butter or margarine, softened
1 cup finely chopped pecans
1 cup pecan halves

1. Preheat oven to 350°F. Grease baking sheets.

2. Combine cake mix, yogurt, egg, butter and chopped pecans in large
bowl. Beat at low speed with electric mixer until blended. Drop by
rounded teaspoonfuls 2 inches apart onto prepared baking sheets.
Press pecan half onto center of each cookie. Bake at 350°F for 11 to
13 minutes or until golden brown. Cool 1 minute on baking sheets.
Remove to cooling racks. Cool completely. Store in airtight container.

Makes 4¹/₂ to 5 dozen cookies

pistachio chip cookies

¹/₂ cup (1 stick) butter
¹/₃ cup light corn syrup
2 tablespoons frozen orange juice concentrate, thawed
1 tablespoon grated orange peel
²/₃ cup packed dark brown sugar
1 cup all-purpose flour
¹/₂ cup chopped pistachio nuts
1 cup (6 ounces) semisweet chocolate chips

Preheat oven to 375°F. Line cookie sheets with foil; lightly grease foil.
Combine butter, corn syrup, orange concentrate, orange peel and sugar
in medium saucepan. Bring to a boil over medium heat, stirring
constantly. Remove from heat; gradually stir in flour and nuts. Cool
completely. Stir in chocolate chips. Drop batter by teaspoonfuls
3 inches apart onto prepared cookie sheets. Bake 8 to 10 minutes or
until golden and lacy. (Cookies are soft when hot, but become crispy
as they cool.) Cool completely on foil, then peel foil from cookies.

Makes about 4 dozen cookies

frosted peanut butter peanut brittle cookies

PEANUT BRITTLE

1½ cups granulated sugar
1½ cups shelled unroasted Spanish peanuts
¾ cup light corn syrup
½ teaspoon salt
1 tablespoon Butter Flavor CRISCO® Stick or 1 tablespoon
Butter Flavor CRISCO® all-vegetable shortening plus
additional for greasing
1½ teaspoons vanilla
1½ teaspoons baking soda

COOKIES

½ Butter Flavor CRISCO® Stick or ½ cup Butter Flavor CRISCO®
all-vegetable shortening
½ cup granulated sugar
½ cup firmly packed brown sugar
½ cup JIF® Creamy Peanut Butter
1 tablespoon milk
1 egg
1⅓ cups all-purpose flour
¾ teaspoon baking soda
½ teaspoon baking powder
¼ teaspoon salt

TOPPING

1¼ cups peanut butter chips
1 cup reserved crushed peanut brittle

1. For peanut brittle, grease 15½×12-inch baking sheet with shortening.

2. Combine 1½ cups granulated sugar, nuts, corn syrup and ½ teaspoon salt in 3-quart saucepan. Cook and stir on medium-low heat until 240°F on candy thermometer.

3. Stir in 1 tablespoon shortening and vanilla. Cook and stir until 300°F on candy thermometer. *Watch closely so mixture does not burn.*

4. Remove from heat. Stir in 1½ teaspoons baking soda. Pour onto prepared baking sheet. Spread to ¼-inch thickness. Cool. Break into pieces. Crush into medium-fine pieces to measure 1 cup. Set aside.

5. For cookies, heat oven to 375°F. Place sheets of foil on countertop for cooling cookies.

6. Combine ½ cup shortening, ½ cup granulated sugar, brown sugar, peanut butter and milk in large bowl. Beat at medium speed of electric mixer until well blended. Beat in egg.

7. Combine flour, ¾ teaspoon baking soda, baking powder and ¼ teaspoon salt. Add gradually at low speed. Mix until well blended.

8. Shape dough into 1¼-inch balls. Place 3½ inches apart on ungreased baking sheet. Flatten into 3-inch circles.

9. Bake for 8 to 9 minutes or until light brown. *Do not overbake.* Cool 2 minutes on baking sheet. Remove cookies to foil to cool completely.

10. For topping, place peanut butter chips in microwave-safe bowl. Microwave at 50% (MEDIUM). Stir after 1 minute. Repeat until smooth (or melt in saucepan on very low heat.) Spread over half of each cookie.

11. Sprinkle reserved crushed peanut brittle over topping. Refrigerate to set quickly or let stand at room temperature.

Makes 2 dozen cookies

Peanuts are not actually nuts—they are legumes. Like nuts, peanuts are quite perishable. Unshelled peanuts can be kept refrigerated for about six months. Unopened, vacuum-packed jars of shelled peanuts can be kept at room temperature for about a year. Once opened and/or shelled, store peanuts in the refrigerator and use them within 3 months.

waikiki cookies

1½ cups packed light brown sugar
⅔ cup shortening
1 tablespoon water
1 teaspoon vanilla
2 eggs
1¾ cups all-purpose flour
½ teaspoon salt
¼ teaspoon baking soda
1 cup white chocolate chunks
1 cup macadamia nuts, coarsely chopped

1. Preheat oven to 375°F.

2. Combine brown sugar, shortening, water and vanilla in large bowl. Beat at medium speed of electric mixer until well blended. Add eggs; beat well.

3. Combine flour, salt and baking soda in medium bowl. Add to sugar mixture; beat at low speed just until blended. Stir in white chocolate chunks and nuts.

4. Drop dough by rounded tablespoonfuls 2 inches apart onto ungreased baking sheet.

5. Bake 7 to 9 minutes or until cookies are set. Do not overbake. Cool 2 minutes on baking sheet. Remove cookies to wire rack; cool completely.   *Makes about 3 dozen cookies*

 If you run out of time before you bake all the cookies in a batch, don't despair. Drop cookie dough may be frozen. Simply drop the dough onto cookie sheets as directed in the recipe and then place in the freezer until the cookies are frozen solid. Then transfer the frozen cookie drops to air-tight, freezer-proof wrapping. Let them thaw about 30 minutes on a cookie sheet at room temperature before baking.

choco-coco pecan crisps

$1/2$ cup (1 stick) butter, softened
1 cup packed light brown sugar
1 egg
1 teaspoon vanilla
$1^{1}/_{2}$ cups all-purpose flour
1 cup chopped pecans
$1/3$ cup unsweetened cocoa powder
$1/2$ teaspoon baking soda
1 cup flaked coconut

Cream butter and brown sugar in large bowl until light and fluffy. Beat in egg and vanilla. Combine flour, pecans, cocoa and baking soda in small bowl until well blended. Add to creamed mixture, blending until stiff dough is formed. Sprinkle coconut on work surface. Divide dough into 4 parts. Shape each part into roll about $1^{1}/_{2}$ inches in diameter; roll in coconut until thickly coated. Wrap in plastic wrap; refrigerate until firm, at least 1 hour or up to 2 weeks. (For longer storage, freeze up to 6 weeks.)

Preheat oven to 350°F. Cut rolls into $1/8$-inch-thick slices. Place 2 inches apart on ungreased cookie sheets. Bake 10 to 13 minutes or until firm, but not overly browned. Remove to wire racks to cool.

Makes about 6 dozen cookies

fruit & nut molasses crescents

- 1 package (18 ounces) refrigerated sugar cookie dough
- 2 tablespoons dark molasses
- 2 tablespoons packed brown sugar
- 6 tablespoons all-purpose flour
- ½ teaspoon ground cinnamon
- ½ teaspoon ground ginger
- 1¼ cups trail mix with nuts, raisins and candy-coated chocolate pieces, coarsely chopped
  Melted white or dark chocolate (optional)

1. Preheat oven to 325°F. Grease cookie sheets. Remove dough from wrapper; place in large bowl. Let dough stand at room temperature about 15 minutes.

2. Add molasses, 2 tablespoons brown sugar, flour, ½ teaspoon cinnamon and ginger to dough in bowl; beat at medium speed of electric mixer until well blended. Divide dough into 4 equal pieces. Wrap pieces individually in plastic wrap and refrigerate at least 2 hours.

3. Roll 1 dough piece into 7-inch circle on lightly floured surface. Sprinkle with 5 tablespoons trail mix. Cut dough into 5 wedges. Roll each wedge from wide end in towards point. Gently shape into crescent. Place crescents 2 inches apart on cookie sheets. Fill sides of crescents with any trail mix that spills out. Repeat with remaining dough and trail mix to make 20 crescents.

4. Bake 12 to 15 minutes or until crescents are lightly browned. Cool on cookie sheets 5 minutes. Place waxed paper under wire racks. Remove crescents to wire racks. Drizzle with melted chocolate, if desired. Let stand until set.   *Makes 20 crescents*

hawaiian drops

$^3/_4$ cup (1$^1/_2$ sticks) butter or margarine, softened
$^3/_4$ cup granulated sugar
$^3/_4$ cup firmly packed light brown sugar
2 large eggs
1 teaspoon vanilla extract
2 cups quick-cooking or old-fashioned oats, uncooked
1$^1/_2$ cups all-purpose flour
1 teaspoon baking powder
1 teaspoon baking soda
1$^3/_4$ cups "M&M's"® Chocolate Mini Baking Bits
1 cup shredded coconut
1 cup coarsely chopped macadamia nuts

Preheat oven to 350°F. Cream butter and sugars until light and fluffy; beat in eggs and vanilla. Combine oats, flour, baking powder and baking soda; blend into creamed mixture. Stir in remaining ingredients. Drop by rounded tablespoonfuls onto greased cookie sheets. Bake 13 to 15 minutes or until edges are golden brown. Cool 1 minute on cookie sheets; cool completely on wire racks. Store in tightly covered container.   *Makes about 6 dozen cookies*

To make chopping nuts easier, warm them first in the microwave (especially if they've been stored refrigerated or frozen). Place 1 cup of shelled nuts in a microwavable dish and heat at HIGH about 30 seconds or just until warm; chop as desired. A food processor may be used to chop nuts. Just place 1 cup of nuts in the bowl with a metal blade. Process using short pulses until the desired texture is reached. Be careful not to overdo it, or you'll create nut butter.

peanut butter thumbprints

1¼ cups firmly packed light brown sugar
¾ cup JIF® Creamy Peanut Butter
½ CRISCO® Stick or ½ cup CRISCO® all-vegetable shortening
3 tablespoons milk
1 tablespoon vanilla
1 egg
1¾ cups all-purpose flour
¾ teaspoon baking soda
¾ teaspoon salt
   Granulated sugar
¼ cup SMUCKER'S® Strawberry Jam, stirred

1. Heat oven to 375°F. Place sheets of foil on countertop for cooling cookies.

2. Place brown sugar, peanut butter, ½ cup shortening, milk and vanilla in large bowl. Beat at medium speed of electric mixer until well blended. Add egg; beat just until blended.

3. Combine flour, baking soda and salt. Add to shortening mixture; beat at low speed just until blended.

4. Shape dough into 1-inch balls. Roll in granulated sugar. Place 2 inches apart on ungreased cookie sheets.

5. Bake one cookie sheet at a time at 375°F for 6 minutes. Press centers of cookies immediately with back of measuring teaspoon. Bake 3 minutes longer or until cookies are set and just beginning to brown. *Do not overbake.* Cool 2 minutes on baking sheet. Spoon jam into center of each cookie. Remove cookies to foil to cool completely.

Makes about 4 dozen cookies

double nut chocolate chip cookies →

1 package DUNCAN HINES® Moist Deluxe® Classic Yellow
   Cake Mix
$1/2$ cup butter or margarine, melted
1 egg
1 cup semisweet chocolate chips
$1/2$ cup finely chopped pecans
1 cup sliced almonds, divided

1. Preheat oven to 375°F. Grease baking sheets.

2. Combine cake mix, butter and egg in large bowl. Mix at low speed with electric mixer until just blended. Stir in chocolate chips, pecans and $1/4$ cup almonds. Shape rounded tablespoonfuls of dough into balls. Place remaining $3/4$ cup almonds in shallow bowl. Press tops of cookies into almonds. Place 1 inch apart on prepared baking sheets.

3. Bake at 375°F for 9 to 11 minutes or until lightly browned. Cool 2 minutes on baking sheets. Remove to cooling racks.

Makes 3 to $3^1/2$ dozen cookies

peanutty double chip cookies

$1/2$ cup butter, softened
$3/4$ cup packed light brown sugar
$3/4$ cup granulated sugar
2 eggs
1 teaspoon baking soda
1 teaspoon vanilla
2 cups all-purpose flour
1 cup chunky peanut butter
1 cup (6 ounces) semisweet or milk chocolate chips
1 cup (6 ounces) peanut butter chips

Preheat oven to 350°F. Lightly grease cookie sheets or line with parchment paper. Beat butter and sugars in large bowl until blended. Add eggs, baking soda and vanilla; beat until light. Blend in flour and peanut butter until dough is stiff and smooth. Stir in chocolate and peanut butter chips. Drop dough by teaspoonfuls 2 inches apart onto prepared cookie sheets. Press cookies down with tines of fork to flatten slightly. Bake 12 minutes or until just barely done. *Do not overbake.* Remove to wire racks to cool. *Makes about 5 dozen cookies*

prized peanut butter crunch cookies

  1 Butter Flavor CRISCO® Stick or 1 cup Butter Flavor CRISCO®
     all-vegetable shortening
  2 cups firmly packed brown sugar
  1 cup JIF® Extra Crunchy Peanut Butter
  4 egg whites, lightly beaten
  1 teaspoon vanilla
  2 cups all-purpose flour
  1 teaspoon baking soda
  $\frac{1}{2}$ teaspoon baking powder
  2 cups crisp rice cereal
$1\frac{1}{2}$ cups chopped peanuts
  1 cup quick oats (not instant or old-fashioned)
  1 cup flake coconut

1. Heat oven to 350°F. Place sheets of foil on countertop for cooling cookies.

2. Combine 1 cup shortening, sugar and peanut butter in large bowl. Beat at medium speed of electric mixer until blended. Beat in egg whites and vanilla.

3. Combine flour, baking soda and baking powder. Mix into creamed mixture at low speed until just blended. Stir in, one at a time, rice cereal, nuts, oats and coconut with spoon.

4. Drop rounded measuring tablespoonfuls of dough 2 inches apart onto ungreased baking sheet.

5. Bake at 350°F, one baking sheet at a time, for 8 to 10 minutes, or until set. *Do not overbake.* Remove cookies to foil to cool completely.

Makes about 4 dozen cookies

chocolate cherry bars

1 cup (2 sticks) butter or margarine
¾ cup HERSHEY'S Cocoa or HERSHEY'S Dutch Processed Cocoa
2 cups sugar
4 eggs
1½ cups plus ⅓ cup all-purpose flour, divided
⅓ cup chopped almonds
1 can (14 ounces) sweetened condensed milk (not evaporated milk)
½ teaspoon almond extract
1 cup HERSHEY'S MINI KISSES™ Semi-Sweet or Milk Chocolates
1 cup chopped maraschino cherries, drained

1. Heat oven to 350°F. Generously grease 13×9×2-inch baking pan.

2. Melt butter in large saucepan over low heat; stir in cocoa until smooth. Remove from heat. Add sugar, 3 eggs, 1½ cups flour and almonds; mix well. Pour into prepared pan. Bake 20 minutes.

3. Meanwhile, whisk together remaining 1 egg, remaining ⅓ cup flour, sweetened condensed milk and almond extract. Pour over baked layer; sprinkle Mini Kisses™ and cherries over top. Return to oven.

4. Bake additional 20 to 25 minutes or until set and edges are golden brown. Cool completely in pan on wire rack. Refrigerate until cold, 6 hours or overnight. Cut into bars. Cover; refrigerate leftover bars.

Makes about 48 bars

tip *Unsweetened cocoa is formed by extracting most of the cocoa butter from pure chocolate and grinding the remaining chocolate solids into a powder. "Dutch process" cocoa is unsweetened cocoa that has been treated with an alkali, giving it a darker appearance and a slightly less bitter flavor. In recipes, do not substitute sweetened cocoa, the type that is used for making hot chocolate, for unsweetened cocoa.*

apple crisp cookies

COOKIES

>1 Butter Flavor CRISCO® Stick or 1 cup Butter Flavor CRISCO® all-vegetable shortening plus additional for greasing
>1 cup firmly packed light brown sugar
>1 teaspoon vanilla
>2½ cups oats (quick or old-fashioned, uncooked)
>2¼ cups all-purpose flour
>½ teaspoon baking soda
>½ teaspoon salt
>6 to 8 tablespoons water

TOPPING

>1 can (21 ounces) apple pie filling, finely chopped
>1 cup reserved crumb mixture
>½ cup finely chopped pecans or walnuts

1. Heat oven to 375°F. Grease baking sheet with shortening. Place sheets of foil on countertop for cooling cookies.

2. For cookies, combine shortening, brown sugar and vanilla in large bowl. Beat at medium speed of electric mixer until well blended.

3. Combine oats, flour, baking soda and salt. Add alternately with water to creamed mixture stirring with spoon. Mix well after each addition. (Mixture will be crumbly, but will hold together when shaped into small ball.) Add additional water if necessary. Reserve 1 cup for topping. Shape remaining dough into 1-inch balls. Place 2 inches apart on greased baking sheet. Flatten to ⅛-inch thickness with floured bottom of glass. Smooth edges.

4. Bake at 375°F for 5 to 7 minutes or until light brown around edges and firm. *Do not overbake.* Remove from oven. Cool on baking sheet about 5 minutes.

5. For topping, place 1 measuring teaspoonful of pie filling in center of each cookie. Spread carefully to cover.

6. Combine 1 cup reserved crumbs and nuts in small bowl. Toss until mixed. Sprinkle over apple filling.

7. Return to oven. Bake 5 minutes or until topping is light brown. *Do not overbake.* Cool 2 minutes on baking sheet. Remove cookies to foil to cool completely.   *Makes about 3 dozen cookies*

double lemon delights

2¼ cups all-purpose flour
½ teaspoon baking powder
½ teaspoon salt
1 cup (2 sticks) butter, softened
¾ cup granulated sugar
1 egg
2 tablespoons grated lemon peel, divided
1 teaspoon vanilla
  Additional sugar
1 cup powdered sugar
4 to 5 teaspoons lemon juice

1. Preheat oven to 375°F.

2. Combine flour, baking powder and salt in small bowl; set aside. Beat butter and granulated sugar in large bowl of electric mixer at medium speed until light and fluffy. Beat in egg, 1 tablespoon lemon peel and vanilla until well blended. Gradually beat in flour mixture on low speed until blended.

3. Drop dough by level ¼ cupfuls onto ungreased cookie sheets, spacing 3 inches apart. Flatten dough until 3 inches in diameter with bottom of glass that has been dipped in additional sugar.

4. Bake 12 to 14 minutes or until cookies are just set and edges are golden brown. Cool on cookie sheets 2 minutes; transfer to wire racks. Cool completely.

5. Combine powdered sugar, lemon juice and remaining 1 tablespoon lemon peel in small bowl; drizzle mixture over cookies. Let stand until icing is set. *Makes about 1 dozen (4-inch) cookies*

variation: To make smaller cookies, drop 2 tablespoonfuls dough 2 inches apart on ungreased cookie sheets. Bake 8 to 10 minutes or until cookies are just set and edges are golden brown. Cool on cookie sheets 2 minutes; transfer to wire racks. Cool completely. Continue with Step 5. Makes about 2 dozen cookies

double chocolate cherry cookies

Cookies
- 1¹/₂ **cups firmly packed light brown sugar**
- ²/₃ **CRISCO® Stick or ²/₃ cup CRISCO® all-vegetable shortening**
- 1 **tablespoon water**
- 1 **teaspoon vanilla**
- 2 **eggs**
- 1¹/₂ **cups all-purpose flour**
- ¹/₃ **cup unsweetened cocoa powder**
- ¹/₂ **teaspoon salt**
- ¹/₄ **teaspoon baking soda**
- 30 to 40 **maraschino cherries**

Icing
- ¹/₂ **cup semisweet chocolate chips or white chocolate chips**
- ¹/₂ **teaspoon CRISCO® Stick or CRISCO® all-vegetable shortening**

1. Heat oven to 375°F. Place sheets of foil on countertop for cooling cookies.

2. For cookies, place brown sugar, ²/₃ cup shortening, water and vanilla in large bowl. Beat at medium speed of electric mixer until well blended. Add eggs; beat well.

3. Combine flour, cocoa, salt and baking soda. Add to shortening mixture; beat at low speed just until blended.

4. Shape rounded measuring tablespoonfuls of dough around each maraschino cherry, covering cherry completely. Place cookies 2 inches apart on ungreased baking sheet.

5. Bake one baking sheet at a time at 375°F for 7 to 9 minutes or until cookies are set. *Do not overbake.* Cool 2 minutes on baking sheet. Remove cookies to foil to cool completely.

6. For icing, place chocolate chips and ¹/₂ teaspoon shortening in heavy resealable sandwich bag; seal bag. Microwave at 50% power (MEDIUM) for 1 minute. Knead bag. If necessary, microwave at 50% power another 30 seconds at a time until mixture is smooth when bag is kneaded. Cut small tip off corner of bag; drizzle chocolate over cookies.

Makes about 3 dozen cookies

marvelous macaroons

1 can (8 ounces) DOLE® Crushed Pineapple
1 can (14 ounces) sweetened condensed milk
1 package (7 ounces) flaked coconut
$^1/_2$ cup margarine, melted
$^1/_2$ cup chopped almonds, toasted
1 teaspoon grated lemon peel
$^1/_4$ teaspoon almond extract
1 cup all-purpose flour
1 teaspoon baking powder

• Preheat oven to 350°F. Drain crushed pineapple well, pressing out excess juice with back of spoon. In large bowl, combine drained pineapple, milk, coconut, margarine, almonds, lemon peel and almond extract.

• In small bowl, combine flour and baking powder. Beat into pineapple mixture until blended. Drop heaping tablespoonfuls of dough 1 inch apart onto greased cookie sheets.

• Bake 13 to 15 minutes or until lightly browned. Garnish with whole almonds, if desired. Cool on wire racks. Store in covered container in refrigerator.   *Makes about 3$^1/_2$ dozen cookies*

 Sweetened condensed milk is a canned product that is the result of evaporating about half of the water from whole milk and adding cane sugar or corn syrup to sweeten and preserve the milk.

fabulous fruit bars

1$\frac{1}{2}$ cups all-purpose flour, divided
1$\frac{1}{2}$ cups sugar, divided
$\frac{1}{2}$ cup MOTT'S® Apple Sauce, divided
$\frac{1}{2}$ teaspoon baking powder
2 tablespoons margarine
$\frac{1}{2}$ cup chopped peeled apple
$\frac{1}{2}$ cup chopped dried apricots
$\frac{1}{2}$ cup chopped cranberries
1 whole egg
1 egg white
1 teaspoon lemon juice
$\frac{1}{2}$ teaspoon vanilla extract
1 teaspoon ground cinnamon

1. Preheat oven to 350°F. Spray 13×9-inch baking pan with nonstick cooking spray.

2. In medium bowl, combine 1$\frac{1}{4}$ cups flour, $\frac{1}{2}$ cup sugar, $\frac{1}{3}$ cup apple sauce and baking powder. Cut in margarine with pastry blender or fork until mixture resembles coarse crumbs.

3. In large bowl, combine apple, apricots, cranberries, remaining apple sauce, whole egg, egg white, lemon juice and vanilla.

4. In small bowl, combine remaining 1 cup sugar, $\frac{1}{4}$ cup flour and cinnamon. Add to fruit mixture, stirring just until mixed.

5. Press half of crumb mixture evenly into bottom of prepared pan. Top with fruit mixture. Sprinkle with remaining crumb mixture.

6. Bake 40 minutes or until lightly browned. Broil, 4 inches from heat, 1 to 2 minutes or until golden brown. Cool on wire rack 15 minutes; cut into 16 bars. *Makes 16 servings*

double chocolate cranberry chunkies

1¾ cups all-purpose flour
⅓ cup unsweetened cocoa powder
½ teaspoon baking powder
½ teaspoon salt
1 cup butter, softened
1 cup granulated sugar
½ cup packed brown sugar
1 egg
1 teaspoon vanilla
2 cups semisweet chocolate chunks or large chocolate chips
¾ cup dried cranberries or dried tart cherries
    Additional granulated sugar

1. Preheat oven to 350°F.

2. Combine flour, cocoa, baking powder and salt in small bowl; set aside. Beat butter, 1 cup granulated sugar and brown sugar in large bowl of electric mixer at medium speed until light and fluffy. Beat in egg and vanilla until well blended. Gradually beat in flour mixture on low speed until blended. Stir in chocolate chunks and cranberries.

3. Drop dough by level ¼ cupfuls onto ungreased cookie sheets, spacing 3 inches apart. Flatten dough until 2 inches in diameter with bottom of glass that has been dipped in additional granulated sugar.

4. Bake 11 to 12 minutes or until cookies are set. Cool cookies 2 minutes on cookie sheets; transfer to wire racks. Cool completely.

Makes about 1 dozen (4-inch) cookies

pineapple and white chip drops

    1 cup (2 sticks) butter or margarine, softened
    1 cup sugar
    2 eggs
    $^1/_2$ teaspoon vanilla extract
    1 can (8 ounces) crushed pineapple, with juice
    $3^1/_2$ cups all-purpose flour
    1 teaspoon baking soda
    $^3/_4$ teaspoon ground cinnamon
    $^1/_2$ teaspoon salt
    $^1/_4$ teaspoon ground nutmeg
    1 cup chopped pecans
    $1^2/_3$ cups (10-ounce package) HERSHEY'S Premier White Chips

1. Heat oven to 350°F. Lightly grease cookie sheet.

2. Beat butter and sugar in large bowl until well blended. Add eggs and vanilla; blend well. Blend in pineapple and juice. Stir together flour, baking soda, cinnamon, salt and nutmeg; gradually add to butter mixture, beating until well blended. Stir in pecans and white chips. Drop by tablespoonfuls onto prepared cookie sheet.

3. Bake 10 to 12 minutes or until lightly browned around edges. Remove from cookie sheet to wire rack. Cool completely.

Makes about 5 dozen cookies

blueberry cheesecake bars

  1 package DUNCAN HINES® Bakery-Style Blueberry Streusel
     Muffin Mix
  ¼ cup cold butter or margarine
  ⅓ cup finely chopped pecans
  1 package (8 ounces) cream cheese, softened
  ½ cup sugar
  1 egg
  3 tablespoons lemon juice
  1 teaspoon grated lemon peel

1. Preheat oven to 350°F. Grease 9-inch square baking pan.

2. Rinse blueberries from Mix with cold water and drain; set aside.

3. Place muffin mix in medium bowl; cut in butter with pastry blender or two knives. Stir in pecans. Press into bottom of prepared pan. Bake at 350°F for 15 minutes or until set.

4. Combine cream cheese and sugar in medium bowl. Beat until smooth. Add egg, lemon juice and lemon peel. Beat well. Spread over baked crust. Sprinkle with blueberries. Sprinkle topping packet from Mix over blueberries. Return to oven. Bake at 350°F for 35 to 40 minutes or until filling is set. Cool completely. Refrigerate until ready to serve. Cut into bars.   *Makes about 16 bars*

pineapple-coconut crescents

  2 cups all-purpose flour
  ¼ cup cornstarch
  ¼ teaspoon salt
  1 cup (2 sticks) unsalted butter, softened
  ½ cup granulated sugar
  1 teaspoon vanilla
  ¾ cup lightly toasted coconut
  ½ cup drained crushed pineapple
     Powdered sugar for dusting

1. Sift together flour, cornstarch and salt in medium bowl; set aside.

2. Beat butter, granulated sugar and vanilla until creamy. Gradually add flour mixture, beating until well blended. Stir in coconut and pineapple, do not overmix. Refrigerate dough at least 1 hour or until firm.

3. Preheat oven to 325°F. Shape dough into crescents. Place 2 inches apart on ungreased cookie sheets. Bake 20 minutes or until golden brown. Let cookies cool on cookie sheets 2 minutes. Transfer to wire rack; cool completely. Sprinkle with powdered sugar.

Makes about 30 cookies

macaroon kiss cookies

   $1/3$ cup butter or margarine, softened
   1 package (3 ounces) cream cheese, softened
   $3/4$ cup sugar
   1 egg yolk
   2 teaspoons almond extract
   2 teaspoons orange juice
   $1^{1}/4$ cups all-purpose flour
   2 teaspoons baking powder
   $1/4$ teaspoon salt
   5 cups MOUNDS® Sweetened Coconut Flakes, divided
   48 HERSHEY'S KISSES® Milk Chocolates

1. Beat together butter, cream cheese and sugar in large bowl. Add egg yolk, almond extract and orange juice; beat well. Stir together flour, baking powder and salt; gradually add to butter mixture. Stir in 3 cups coconut. Cover; refrigerate 1 hour or until firm enough to handle. Meanwhile, remove wrappers from chocolate pieces.

2. Heat oven to 350°F. Shape dough into 1-inch balls; roll in remaining 2 cups coconut. Place on ungreased cookie sheets.

3. Bake 10 to 12 minutes or until lightly browned. Remove cookies from oven; immediately press chocolate piece in center of each cookie. Cool 1 minute. Carefully remove from cookie sheets to wire racks. Cool completely.

Makes about 4 dozen cookies

grape-filled cookies

2 cups coarsely chopped California seedless grapes
$1/4$ cup packed brown sugar
$1/2$ teaspoon ground cinnamon
1 teaspoon lemon juice
   Sugar Cookie Dough (recipe follows)

Combine grapes, sugar and cinnamon in saucepan. Bring to a boil; cook and stir over medium heat 35 minutes or until thickened. Stir in lemon juice; cool. Roll Sugar Cookie Dough to $1/8$-inch thickness. Cut into 24 ($2^{1}/_{2}$-inch) circles. Place 12 circles on greased cookie sheet. Place heaping teaspoonful of grape mixture on each circle, leaving $1/8$-inch border around edges. Place remaining circles on filling; press together with fork. Cut 3 to 5 slits through top circles of dough. Bake at 400°F 6 to 8 minutes or until lightly browned. Cool on wire rack.

Makes about 1 dozen cookies

sugar cookie dough: Beat $1/3$ cup butter or margarine and 2 tablespoons sugar until smooth. Beat in 1 egg and $1/2$ teaspoon vanilla. Combine 1 cup all-purpose flour, $3/4$ teaspoon baking powder and dash salt; stir into butter mixture. Wrap and refrigerate at least 1 hour.

Favorite recipe from **California Table Grape Commission**

tip *When rolling out cookie dough, work with only a small amount at a time. Keep the rest refrigerated until needed. You can roll on top of a counter covered with waxed paper. Just put a few tiny drops of water under the paper to keep it in place. You can also spray a clean, smooth countertop with nonstick cooking spray and roll right on it. To keep cookie cutters from sticking to the dough, spray them with cooking spray or dip them in flour or powdered sugar.*

raspberry-filled chocolate ravioli

  1 cup butter, softened
  1/2 cup granulated sugar
  2 squares (1 ounce each) bittersweet or semisweet chocolate,
     melted and cooled
  1 egg
  1 teaspoon vanilla
  1/2 teaspoon chocolate extract
  1/4 teaspoon baking soda
     Dash salt
  2 1/2 cups all-purpose flour
  1 cup seedless raspberry jam
     Powdered sugar

Mix butter and granulated sugar in large bowl until blended. Add melted chocolate, egg, vanilla, chocolate extract, baking soda and salt; beat until light. Blend in flour to make stiff dough. Divide dough in half. Cover; refrigerate until firm.

Preheat oven to 350°F. Lightly grease cookie sheets or line with parchment paper. Roll out dough, half at a time, 1/8 inch thick between two sheets of plastic wrap. Remove top sheet of plastic. (If dough gets too soft and sticks to plastic, refrigerate until firm.) Cut dough into 1 1/2-inch squares. Place half the squares, 2 inches apart, on prepared cookie sheets. Place about 1/2 teaspoon jam on center of each square; top with another square. Using fork, press edges of squares together to seal, then pierce center of each square. Bake 10 minutes or just until edges are browned. Remove to wire racks to cool. Dust lightly with powdered sugar. *Makes about 6 dozen ravioli*

peach oatmeal cookies

¾ **cup granulated sugar**
¾ **cup packed brown sugar**
⅔ **cup margarine**
2 **eggs**
1½ **teaspoons vanilla**
1½ **cups whole wheat flour**
2 **teaspoons baking powder**
1 **teaspoon salt**
2½ **cups rolled oats**
1½ **cups diced peeled fresh California peaches**
1 **cup raisins**

1. Preheat oven to 350°F.

2. Beat sugars, margarine, eggs and vanilla in large mixing bowl with electric mixer at medium speed.

3. Combine flour, baking powder and salt in separate bowl. Add to egg mixture and beat at low speed 2 to 3 minutes or until smooth.

4. Stir in oats, peaches and raisins. Drop by tablespoonfuls onto nonstick baking sheet.

5. Bake 10 to 15 minutes or until golden.   *Makes 3 dozen cookies*

Favorite recipe from **California Tree Fruit Agreement**

Rolled oats are often called old-fashioned oats. They have been steamed and then rolled flat to make them cook more quickly than steel-cut oats (also called Irish oatmeal). Quick cooking oats are cut into smaller pieces before processing and instant oatmeal is actually pre-cooked. Most cookie recipes call for rolled or old-fashioned oats. Do not substitute instant oats or steel-cut oats.

no-bake pineapple marmalade squares

   1 cup graham cracker crumbs
  ½ cup plus 2 tablespoons sugar, divided
  ¼ cup light margarine, melted
   1 cup fat free or light sour cream
   4 ounces light cream cheese, softened
  ¼ cup orange marmalade or apricot fruit spread, divided
   1 can (20 ounces) DOLE® Crushed Pineapple
   1 envelope unflavored gelatin

• Combine graham cracker crumbs, 2 tablespoons sugar and margarine in 8-inch square glass baking dish; pat mixture firmly and evenly onto bottom of dish. Freeze 10 minutes.

• Beat sour cream, cream cheese, remaining 1/2 cup sugar and 1 tablespoon marmalade in medium bowl until smooth and blended; set aside.

• Drain crushed pineapple; reserve 1/4 cup juice.

• Sprinkle gelatin over reserved juice in small saucepan; let stand 1 minute. Cook and stir over low heat until gelatin dissolves.

• Beat gelatin mixture into sour cream mixture until well blended. Spoon mixture evenly over crust.

• Stir together crushed pineapple and remaining 3 tablespoons marmalade in small bowl until blended. Evenly spoon over sour cream filling. Cover and refrigerate 2 hours or until firm.

Makes 16 servings

lemony butter cookies

 $^1/_2$ cup (1 stick) butter, softened
 $^1/_2$ cup sugar
  1 egg
 $1^1/_2$ cups all-purpose flour
  2 tablespoons fresh lemon juice
  1 teaspoon grated lemon peel
 $^1/_2$ teaspoon baking powder
 $^1/_8$ teaspoon salt
    Additional sugar

Beat butter and sugar in large bowl with electric mixer at medium speed until creamy. Beat in egg until light and fluffy. Mix in flour, lemon juice and peel, baking powder and salt. Cover; refrigerate about 2 hours or until firm.

Preheat oven to 350°F. Roll out dough, a small portion at a time, on well-floured surface to $^1/_4$-inch thickness. (Keep remaining dough in refrigerator.) Cut with 3-inch round or fluted cookie cutter. Transfer to ungreased cookie sheets. Sprinkle with sugar.

Bake 8 to 10 minutes or until edges are lightly browned. Cool 1 minute on cookie sheets. Remove to wire racks; cool completely. Store in airtight container.   *Makes about 2$^1/_2$ dozen cookies*

apricot biscotti

  3 cups all-purpose flour
 $1^1/_2$ teaspoons baking soda
 $^1/_2$ teaspoon salt
 $^2/_3$ cup sugar
  3 eggs
  1 teaspoon vanilla
 $^1/_2$ cup chopped dried apricots*
 $^1/_3$ cup sliced almonds, chopped
  1 tablespoon reduced-fat (2%) milk

Other chopped dried fruits, such as dried cherries, cranberries or blueberries, can be substituted.

1. Preheat oven to 350°F. Lightly coat cookie sheet with nonstick cooking spray; set aside.

2. Combine flour, baking soda and salt in medium bowl; set aside.

3. Beat sugar, eggs and vanilla in large bowl with electric mixer at medium speed until combined. Add flour mixture; beat well.

4. Stir in apricots and almonds. Turn dough out onto lightly floured work surface. Knead 4 to 6 times. Shape dough into 20-inch log; place on prepared cookie sheet. Brush dough with milk.

5. Bake 30 minutes or until firm. Remove from oven; cool 10 minutes. Diagonally slice into 30 biscotti. Place slices on cookie sheet. Bake 10 minutes; turn and bake additional 10 minutes. Cool on wire racks. Store in airtight container.   *Makes 2¹/₂ dozen biscotti*

chocolate banana walnut drops

     ¹/₂ cup (1 stick) butter or margarine, softened
     ¹/₂ cup solid vegetable shortening
  1¹/₄ cups firmly packed light brown sugar
     1 large egg
     1 medium banana, mashed (about ¹/₂ cup)
  2¹/₄ cups all-purpose flour
     1 teaspoon baking soda
     1 teaspoon ground cinnamon
     ¹/₂ teaspoon ground nutmeg
     ¹/₄ teaspoon salt
     2 cups quick-cooking or old-fashioned oats, uncooked
     1 cup coarsely chopped walnuts
  1³/₄ cups "M&M's"® Chocolate Mini Baking Bits

Preheat oven to 350°F. In large bowl cream butter, shortening and sugar until light and fluffy; beat in egg and banana. In medium bowl combine flour, baking soda, cinnamon, nutmeg and salt; blend into creamed mixture. Blend in oats and nuts. Stir in "M&M's"® Chocolate Mini Baking Bits. Drop by tablespoonfuls about 2 inches apart onto ungreased cookie sheets. Bake 8 to 10 minutes just until set. Do not overbake. Cool 1 minute on cookie sheets; cool completely on wire racks. Store in tightly covered container.

Makes about 3 dozen cookies

quick
cookies

no-bake chocolate peanut butter bars

2 cups peanut butter, *divided*
¾ cup (1½ sticks) butter, softened
2 cups powdered sugar, *divided*
3 cups graham cracker crumbs
2 cups (12-ounce package) NESTLÉ® TOLL HOUSE® Semi-Sweet
    Chocolate Mini Morsels, *divided*

GREASE 13×9-inch baking pan.

BEAT 1¼ cups peanut butter and butter in large mixer bowl until creamy. Gradually beat in *1 cup* powdered sugar. With hands or wooden spoon, work in *remaining* powdered sugar, graham cracker crumbs and ½ *cup* morsels. Press evenly into prepared pan. Smooth top with spatula.

MELT *remaining* peanut butter and *remaining* morsels in medium, *heavy-duty* saucepan over *lowest possible heat,* stirring constantly, until smooth. Spread over graham cracker crust in pan. Refrigerate for at least 1 hour or until chocolate is firm; cut into bars. Store in refrigerator. *Makes 5 dozen bars*

To quickly soften butter, you can cut it into smaller pieces or even grate it on your box grater. The microwave also works well. Just place 1 stick of butter on a microwavable plate and heat at LOW (30% power) about 30 seconds or until softened.

easy microwave brownies

    1 cup granulated sugar
   1/4 cup packed light brown sugar
   1/2 cup vegetable oil
    2 eggs
    2 tablespoons light corn syrup
 1 1/2 teaspoons vanilla
    1 cup all-purpose flour
   1/2 cup unsweetened cocoa powder
   1/4 teaspoon baking powder
   1/4 teaspoon salt
   1/2 cup powdered sugar

Microwave Directions

1. Lightly grease 8×8-inch microwavable baking pan.

2. Combine granulated sugar, brown sugar, oil, eggs, corn syrup and vanilla in large bowl. Combine flour, cocoa, baking powder and salt in medium bowl. Add flour mixture to sugar mixture; blend well. Spread batter in prepared pan.

3. Microwave at MEDIUM-HIGH (70% power) 3 minutes. Rotate pan 1/2 turn; microwave at MEDIUM-HIGH 3 minutes or until brownies begin to pull away from sides of pan and surface has no wet spots. (If brownies are not done, rotate pan 1/4 turn and continue to microwave at MEDIUM-HIGH, checking for doneness at 30-second intervals.) Let brownies stand 20 minutes. When cool, sprinkle with powdered sugar and cut into squares. *Makes about 16 brownies*

butterscotch crispies

2 cups sifted all-purpose flour
1 teaspoon baking soda
1 teaspoon salt
$^1/_2$ cup margarine
$2^1/_2$ cups packed light brown sugar
2 eggs
1 teaspoon vanilla extract
2 cups quick-cooking rolled oats
2 cups puffed rice cereal
$^1/_2$ cup chopped walnuts

Preheat oven to 350°F. Sift flour, baking soda and salt onto waxed paper. Cream margarine and brown sugar with electric mixer at medium speed in large bowl until fluffy. Beat in eggs, 1 at a time, until fluffy. Stir in vanilla.

Add flour mixture, $^1/_3$ at a time, until well blended; stir in rolled oats, rice cereal and walnuts. Drop by teaspoonfuls, about 1 inch apart, onto large cookie sheets lightly sprayed with nonstick cooking spray. Bake 10 minutes or until cookies are firm and lightly golden. Remove to wire racks; cool.   *Makes 8$^1/_2$ dozen cookies*

Favorite recipe from **The Sugar Association, Inc.**

 Although today most all-purpose flour comes pre-sifted, flour can settle and compact. When recipes indicate that flour should be sifted before measuring, like the one above, it's important to take the extra step for best results. Four cups sifted flour equals about 3$^1/_3$ cups unsifted flour, so it can make a substantial difference.

fudge-filled bars

1 (14-ounce) can EAGLE BRAND® Sweetened Condensed Milk
   (NOT evaporated milk)
1 (12-ounce) package semi-sweet chocolate chips
2 tablespoons butter or margarine
2 teaspoons vanilla extract
2 (18-ounce) packages refrigerated cookie dough (oatmeal-
   chocolate chip, chocolate chip or sugar cookie dough)

1. Preheat oven to 350°F. In heavy saucepan over medium heat, combine Eagle Brand, chips and butter; heat until chips melt, stirring often. Remove from heat; stir in vanilla. Cool 15 minutes.

2. Using floured hands, press 1½ packages of cookie dough into ungreased 15×10×1-inch baking pan. Pour cooled chocolate mixture evenly over dough. Crumble remaining dough over chocolate mixture.

3. Bake 25 to 30 minutes. Cool. Cut into bars. Store covered at room temperature. *Makes 48 bars*

helpful hint: If you want to trim the fat in any Eagle Brand recipe, just use Eagle Brand® Fat Free or Low Fat Sweetened Condensed Milk instead of the original Eagle Brand.

Prep Time: 20 minutes
Bake Time: 25 to 30 minutes

magic make it your way drop cookies

3 cups sifted all-purpose flour
3 teaspoons baking powder
³/₄ teaspoon salt
³/₄ cup (1¹/₂ sticks) butter or margarine, softened
2 eggs
1 teaspoon vanilla extract
1 (14-ounce) can EAGLE BRAND® Sweetened Condensed Milk
   (NOT evaporated milk)
One "favorite" ingredient (see below)

1. Preheat oven to 350°F. Grease baking sheets; set aside. In large mixing bowl, sift together dry ingredients. Stir in butter, eggs, vanilla and Eagle Brand. Fold in one of your "favorite" ingredients.

2. Drop by level teaspoonfuls, about 2 inches apart, onto prepared baking sheets. Bake 8 to 10 minutes or until edges are lightly browned. Remove at once from baking sheet. Cool. Store covered at room temperature. *Makes about 4 dozen cookies*

"make it your way" with your favorite ingredient (pick one):
1 (6-ounce) package semi-sweet chocolate chips, 1¹/₂ cups raisins, 1¹/₂ cups corn flakes, 1¹/₂ cups toasted shredded coconut

Prep Time: 15 minutes
Bake Time: 8 to 10 minutes

Top to bottom: *Magic Make It Your Way Drop Cookies, Versatile Cut-Out Cookies (page 140)*

versatile cut-out cookies

3⅓ cups all-purpose flour
1 tablespoon baking powder
½ teaspoon salt
1 (14-ounce) can EAGLE BRAND® Sweetened Condensed Milk
   (NOT evaporated milk)
¾ cup (1½ sticks) butter or margarine, softened
2 eggs
2 teaspoons vanilla *or* 1½ teaspoons almond or lemon extract
Favorite EAGLE BRAND® frosting recipe or ready-to-spread
   frosting, if desired
Colored sprinkles and sugars

1. Preheat oven to 350°F. Grease baking sheets; set aside. In medium mixing bowl, combine flour, baking powder and salt; set aside. In large mixing bowl, beat Eagle Brand, butter, eggs and vanilla until well blended. Add dry ingredients; mix well.

2. On floured surface, lightly knead dough to form smooth ball. Divide into thirds. On well-floured surface, roll out each portion to ⅛-inch thickness. Cut with floured cookie cutter. Place 1 inch apart on prepared sheets.

3. Bake 7 to 9 minutes or until lightly browned around edges. Cool completely. Prepare your favorite Eagle Brand frosting, if desired. Frost and decorate cookies as desired. Store loosely covered at room temperature. *Makes about 6½ dozen cookies*

sandwich cookies: Prepare and bake cookies as directed above using 2½-inch cookie cutter. Sandwich two cookies together with frosting. Sprinkle with powdered sugar or colored sugar, if desired. Makes about 3 dozen sandwich cookies.

Prep Time: 15 minutes
Bake Time: 7 to 9 minutes

peanut butter cereal bars

3 cups miniature marshmallows
3 tablespoons margarine
$\frac{1}{2}$ cup reduced-fat peanut butter
3$\frac{1}{2}$ cups crisp rice cereal
1 cup uncooked quick oats
$\frac{1}{3}$ cup mini semisweet chocolate chips

1. Lightly coat 13×9-inch baking pan with nonstick cooking spray; set aside.

2. Combine marshmallows and margarine in large microwavable bowl. Microwave at HIGH 15 seconds; stir. Continue to microwave 1 minute; stir until marshmallows are melted and mixture is smooth. Add peanut butter; stir. Add cereal and oats; stir until well coated. Spread into prepared pan. Immediately sprinkle chocolate chips on top; lightly press.

3. Cool completely in pan. Cut into 40 bars.   *Makes 40 servings*

tip: To make spreading the cereal mixture easier and cleanup a snap, lightly spray your spoon with nonstick cooking spray before stirring these bars.

quick and easy jumbles

1 package (about 17 ounces) sugar cookie mix
$\frac{1}{2}$ cup butter, melted
1 egg, lightly beaten
$\frac{1}{2}$ cup mini candy-coated chocolate pieces *or* $\frac{1}{2}$ cup semisweet chocolate chips
$\frac{1}{2}$ cup raisins
$\frac{1}{2}$ cup coarsely chopped walnuts

1. Preheat oven to 350°F.

2. Combine cookie mix, butter and egg in large bowl. Stir with spoon until well blended. Stir in chocolate pieces, raisins and walnuts.

3. Drop dough by rounded teaspoonfuls onto *ungreased* cookie sheets about 2 inches apart. Bake for 7 to 8 minutes or until set. Cool 1 minute on sheets. Remove cookies to wire racks; cool completely.
Makes about 2 dozen cookies

irresistible peanut butter cookies

1¼ **cups firmly packed light brown sugar**
¾ **cup JIF® Creamy Peanut Butter**
½ **Butter Flavor CRISCO® Stick or ½ cup Butter Flavor CRISCO®**
   all-vegetable shortening
3 **tablespoons milk**
1 **tablespoon vanilla**
1 **egg**
1¾ **cups all-purpose flour**
¾ **teaspoon baking soda**
¾ **teaspoon salt**

1. Heat oven to 375°F. Place sheets of foil on countertop for cooling cookies.

2. Combine brown sugar, peanut butter, ½ cup shortening, milk and vanilla in large bowl. Beat at medium speed of electric mixer until well blended. Add egg. Beat just until blended.

3. Combine flour, baking soda and salt. Add to creamed mixture at low speed. Mix just until blended.

4. Drop by rounded measuring tablespoonfuls of dough 2 inches apart onto ungreased baking sheet. Flatten slightly in crisscross pattern with tines of fork.

5. Bake one baking sheet at a time at 375°F for 7 to 8 minutes, or until set and just beginning to brown. *Do not overbake.* Cool 2 minutes on baking sheet. Remove cookies to foil to cool completely.

Makes about 3 dozen cookies

quick fruit & lemon drops →

    1 package (18¼ ounces) lemon cake mix
¼ **cup water**
¼ **cup butter, softened**
  1 egg
  1 tablespoon grated lemon peel
  1 cup mixed dried fruit bits
½ **cup sugar**

1. Preheat oven to 350°F. Grease cookie sheets.

2. Beat cake mix, water, butter, egg and lemon peel in large bowl of electric mixer at low speed until well blended. Beat in fruit bits just until blended.

3. Place sugar in small bowl. Roll 1 heaping tablespoon dough into ball; roll in sugar. Repeat with remaining dough. Place 2 inches apart on prepared cookie sheets.

4. Bake 12 to 14 minutes or until set. Let stand on cookie sheets 2 minutes. Transfer to wire racks; cool completely.

Makes about 2 dozen cookies

tip: if dough is too wet add about ¼ cup all-purpose flour.

quick chocolate softies

    1 package (about 18 ounces) devil's food cake mix
⅓ **cup water**
¼ **cup butter, softened**
  1 egg
  1 cup white chocolate chips
½ **cup coarsely chopped walnuts**

Preheat oven to 350°F. Grease cookie sheets. Combine cake mix, water, butter and egg in large bowl. Beat with electric mixer at low speed until moistened. Increase speed to medium; beat 1 minute. (Dough will be thick.) Stir in white chocolate chips and nuts; mix until well blended. Drop dough by heaping teaspoonfuls 2 inches apart onto prepared cookie sheets.

Bake 10 to 12 minutes or until set. Let cookies stand on cookie sheets 1 minute. Remove cookies to wire racks; cool completely.

Makes about 4 dozen cookies

chocolate oat chewies →

1 package DUNCAN HINES® Moist Deluxe® Devil's Food
   Cake Mix
1¹⁄₃ cups old-fashioned oats, uncooked
1 cup flaked coconut, toasted and divided
³⁄₄ cup butter or margarine, melted
2 eggs, beaten
1 teaspoon vanilla extract
5 bars (1.55 ounces each) milk chocolate, cut into rectangles

1. Preheat oven to 350°F.

2. Combine cake mix, oats, ¹⁄₂ cup coconut, butter, eggs and vanilla extract in large bowl. Cover and chill 15 minutes.

3. Shape dough into 1-inch balls. Place balls 2 inches apart on ungreased baking sheets. Bake at 350°F for 12 minutes or until tops are slightly cracked. Remove from oven. Press one milk chocolate rectangle into center of each cookie. Sprinkle with remaining ¹⁄₂ cup coconut. Remove to cooling racks.   *Makes about 4¹⁄₂ dozen cookies*

no-bake cherry crisps

¹⁄₄ cup butter, softened
1 cup powdered sugar
1 cup peanut butter
1¹⁄₃ cups crisp rice cereal
¹⁄₂ cup maraschino cherries, drained, dried and chopped
¹⁄₄ cup plus 2 tablespoons mini semisweet chocolate chips
¹⁄₄ cup chopped pecans
1 to 2 cups flaked coconut (for rolling)

Beat butter, powdered sugar and peanut butter in large bowl. Stir in cereal, cherries, chocolate chips and pecans. Mix well. Shape teaspoonfuls of dough into 1-inch balls. Roll in coconut. Place on cookie sheets and refrigerate 1 hour. Store in refrigerator.

Makes about 3 dozen cookies

red's ultimate "m&m's"® cookies

  1 cup (2 sticks) butter, softened
  ½ cup granulated sugar
  ½ cup firmly packed light brown sugar
  1 large egg
  1 teaspoon vanilla extract
  2 cups all-purpose flour
  ½ teaspoon baking soda
  ⅛ teaspoon salt
  2 cups "M&M's"® Milk Chocolate Mini Baking Bits
  ¾ cup chopped nuts, optional

Preheat oven to 350° F. In large bowl cream butter and sugars until light and fluffy; beat in egg and vanilla. In medium bowl combine flour, baking soda and salt; blend into creamed mixture. Stir in "M&M's"® Milk Chocolate Mini Baking Bits and nuts, if desired. Drop by heaping tablespoonfuls about 2 inches apart onto ungreased cookie sheets. Bake 10 to 13 minutes or until edges are lightly browned and centers are still soft. Do not overbake. Cool 1 minute on cookie sheets; cool completely on wire racks. Store in tightly covered container.

Makes about 3 dozen cookies

white chocolate triangles

  1 cup white chocolate chips
  ½ cup sweetened condensed milk
  ½ cup toasted chopped pecans
  ½ (9-ounce) package chocolate wafers, crushed

1. Grease 8×8-inch baking pan. Combine chips and condensed milk in saucepan; cook and stir over low heat until chips are melted. Stir in pecans and wafer crumbs.

2. Spread mixture in prepared pan; let stand until set. Cut into triangles and store tightly covered in refrigerator. Serve chilled or at room temperature.

Makes 72 triangles

orange pecan cookies

1 package (about 17 ounces) sugar cookie mix
1/2 cup butter, melted
1 egg, lightly beaten
1 teaspoon grated orange peel
1/2 cup chopped pecans
1/2 cup powdered sugar
1 1/2 teaspoons orange juice

1. Preheat oven to 375° F. Blend cookie mix, butter, egg and orange peel in large bowl. Stir in pecans. Drop dough by rounded teaspoonfuls onto *ungreased* cookie sheets about 2 inches apart. Bake for 7 to 8 minutes or until set. Cool 1 minute on cookie sheets. Remove to wire racks; cool completely.

2. Combine powdered sugar and orange juice in small bowl; stir until well blended. Drizzle over top of cooled cookies. Allow glaze to set before storing between layers of waxed paper in airtight container.
Makes about 3 dozen cookies

crispy's irresistible peanut butter marbles

1 package (18 ounces) refrigerated peanut butter cookie dough
2 cups "M&M's"® Milk Chocolate Mini Baking Bits, divided
1 cup crisp rice cereal, divided (optional)
1 package (18 ounces) refrigerated sugar cookie dough
1/4 cup unsweetened cocoa powder

In large bowl combine peanut butter dough, 1 cup "M&M's"® Milk Chocolate Mini Baking Bits and 1/2 cup cereal, if desired. Remove dough to small bowl; set aside. In large bowl blend sugar dough and cocoa powder. Stir in remaining 1 cup "M&M's"® and remaining 1/2 cup cereal, if desired. Remove half the dough to small bowl; set aside. Combine half the peanut butter dough with half the chocolate dough by folding together just enough to marble. Shape marbled dough into 8×2-inch log. Wrap log in plastic wrap. Repeat with remaining doughs. Refrigerate logs 2 hours. Preheat oven to 350° F. Cut dough into 1/2-inch-thick slices. Place 2 inches apart on ungreased cookie sheets. Bake 12 to 15 minutes. Cool 1 minute on cookie sheets; cool completely on wire racks. *Makes about 5 dozen cookies*

marshmallow krispie bars →

1 (21-ounce) package DUNCAN HINES® Family-Style Chewy
   Fudge Brownie Mix
1 package (10$\frac{1}{2}$ ounces) miniature marshmallows
1$\frac{1}{2}$ cups semisweet chocolate chips
1 cup creamy peanut butter
1 tablespoon butter or margarine
1$\frac{1}{2}$ cups crisp rice cereal

1. Preheat oven to 350°F. Grease bottom only of 13×9-inch pan.

2. Prepare and bake brownies following package directions for cake-like recipe. Remove from oven. Sprinkle marshmallows on hot brownies. Return to oven. Bake for 3 minutes longer.

3. Place chocolate chips, peanut butter and butter in medium saucepan. Cook over low heat, stirring constantly, until chips are melted. Add rice cereal; mix well. Spread mixture over marshmallow layer. Refrigerate until chilled. Cut into bars.

Makes about 2 dozen bars

tip: For a special presentation, cut bars into diamond shapes.

peanut butter & banana cookies

$\frac{1}{4}$ cup butter
$\frac{1}{2}$ cup mashed ripe banana
$\frac{1}{2}$ cup no-sugar-added natural peanut butter
$\frac{1}{4}$ cup thawed frozen unsweetened apple juice concentrate
1 egg
1 teaspoon vanilla
1 cup all-purpose flour
$\frac{1}{2}$ teaspoon baking soda
$\frac{1}{4}$ teaspoon salt
$\frac{1}{2}$ cup chopped salted peanuts

Preheat oven to 375°F. Beat butter in large bowl until creamy. Add banana and peanut butter; beat until smooth. Blend in apple juice concentrate, egg and vanilla. Beat in flour, baking soda and salt. Stir in chopped peanuts. Drop rounded tablespoonfuls of dough 2 inches apart onto lightly greased cookie sheets. Bake 8 minutes or until set. Cool completely on wire racks. Store in tightly covered container.

Makes 2 dozen cookies

double delicious cookie bars →

½ cup (1 stick) butter or margarine
1½ cups graham cracker crumbs
1 (14-ounce) can EAGLE BRAND® Sweetened Condensed Milk
   (NOT evaporated milk)
2 cups (12 ounces) semi-sweet chocolate chips*
1 cup (6 ounces) peanut butter-flavored chips*

*Butterscotch-flavored chips or white chocolate chips can be substituted for the semi-sweet chocolate chips and/or peanut butter-flavored chips.

1. Preheat oven to 350°F (325°F for glass dish). In 13×9-inch baking pan, melt butter in oven.

2. Sprinkle crumbs evenly over butter; pour Eagle Brand evenly over crumbs. Top with remaining ingredients; press down firmly.

3. Bake 25 to 30 minutes or until lightly browned. Cool. Cut into bars. Store covered at room temperature.   *Makes 2 to 3 dozen bars*

Prep Time: 10 minutes
Bake Time: 25 to 30 minutes

toffee bars

½ cup butter, softened
½ cup packed light brown sugar
1 egg yolk
1 teaspoon vanilla
1 cup all-purpose flour
1 cup (6 ounces) milk chocolate chips
½ cup chopped walnuts or pecans

Preheat oven to 350°F. Lightly grease a 13×9-inch pan. Cream butter and sugar in large bowl. Blend in egg yolk and vanilla. Stir in flour until well blended. Press on bottom of prepared pan. Bake 15 minutes or until golden. Remove from oven; sprinkle chocolate chips over the top. Let stand a few minutes until chips melt, then spread evenly over bars. Sprinkle nuts over chocolate. Score into 2×1½-inch bars while still warm. Cool completely in pan on wire rack before cutting and removing from pan.   *Makes about 3 dozen bars*

easy turtle squares

1 package (about 18 ounces) chocolate cake mix
$^{1}/_{2}$ cup butter, melted
$^{1}/_{4}$ cup milk
1 cup (6-ounce package) semisweet chocolate chips
1 cup chopped pecans, divided
1 jar (12 ounces) caramel ice cream topping

1. Preheat oven to 350°F. Spray 13×9-inch pan with nonstick cooking spray.

2. Combine cake mix, butter and milk in large bowl. Press half of mixture into prepared pan.

3. Bake 7 to 8 minutes or until batter begins to form crust. Carefully remove from oven. Sprinkle chocolate chips and $^{1}/_{2}$ cup pecans over partially baked crust. Drizzle caramel topping over chips and pecans. Drop spoonfuls of remaining cake batter over caramel mixture; sprinkle with remaining $^{1}/_{2}$ cup pecans.

4. Return to oven; bake 18 to 20 minutes longer or until top of cake layer springs back when lightly touched. (Caramel center will be soft.) Cool completely on wire rack. Cut into squares.

Makes 24 bar cookies

Oven temperatures can vary significantly, so it's worth investing in an oven thermometer. That way you'll be able to adjust the temperature on the dial to the reality inside. Baked goods will have less chance of being over-browned or under-done. It's fine to leave the thermometer in the oven all the time, but if your oven is self cleaning, remember to remove it during cleaning cycles.

acknowledgments

*The publisher would like to thank the companies and organizations
listed below for the use of their recipes and photographs
in this publication.*

California Table Grape Commission

California Tree Fruit Agreement

Dole Food Company, Inc.

Duncan Hines® and Moist Deluxe® are registered trademarks of
Aurora Foods Inc.

Eagle Brand®

Hershey Foods Corporation

© Mars, Incorporated 2004

Mott's® is a registered trademark of Mott's, Inc.

Nestlé USA

The J.M. Smucker Company

Sokol and Company

The Sugar Association, Inc.

Unilever Bestfoods North America

Washington Apple Commission

index

METRIC CONVERSION CHART

VOLUME MEASUREMENTS (dry)

$1/8$ teaspoon = 0.5 mL
$1/4$ teaspoon = 1 mL
$1/2$ teaspoon = 2 mL
$3/4$ teaspoon = 4 mL
1 teaspoon = 5 mL
1 tablespoon = 15 mL
2 tablespoons = 30 mL
$1/4$ cup = 60 mL
$1/3$ cup = 75 mL
$1/2$ cup = 125 mL
$2/3$ cup = 150 mL
$3/4$ cup = 175 mL
1 cup = 250 mL
2 cups = 1 pint = 500 mL
3 cups = 750 mL
4 cups = 1 quart = 1 L

VOLUME MEASUREMENTS (fluid)

1 fluid ounce (2 tablespoons) = 30 mL
4 fluid ounces ($1/2$ cup) = 125 mL
8 fluid ounces (1 cup) = 250 mL
12 fluid ounces ($1 1/2$ cups) = 375 mL
16 fluid ounces (2 cups) = 500 mL

WEIGHTS (mass)

$1/2$ ounce = 15 g
1 ounce = 30 g
3 ounces = 90 g
4 ounces = 120 g
8 ounces = 225 g
10 ounces = 285 g
12 ounces = 360 g
16 ounces = 1 pound = 450 g

DIMENSIONS

$1/16$ inch = 2 mm
$1/8$ inch = 3 mm
$1/4$ inch = 6 mm
$1/2$ inch = 1.5 cm
$3/4$ inch = 2 cm
1 inch = 2.5 cm

OVEN TEMPERATURES

250°F = 120°C
275°F = 140°C
300°F = 150°C
325°F = 160°C
350°F = 180°C
375°F = 190°C
400°F = 200°C
425°F = 220°C
450°F = 230°C

BAKING PAN SIZES

Utensil	Size in Inches/Quarts	Metric Volume	Size in Centimeters
Baking or Cake Pan (square or rectangular)	8×8×2	2 L	20×20×5
	9×9×2	2.5 L	23×23×5
	12×8×2	3 L	30×20×5
	13×9×2	3.5 L	33×23×5
Loaf Pan	8×4×3	1.5 L	20×10×7
	9×5×3	2 L	23×13×7
Round Layer Cake Pan	8×1½	1.2 L	20×4
	9×1½	1.5 L	23×4
Pie Plate	8×1¼	750 mL	20×3
	9×1¼	1 L	23×3
Baking Dish or Casserole	1 quart	1 L	—
	1½ quart	1.5 L	—
	2 quart	2 L	—